Control. Move. Dominate.

The True Story of the Morning Glory Boys

By

Larry Barnhill

with Jerry Payne

BnB Holdings Publishing, LLC

In association with Broader Thoughts Production, LLC

Control. Move. Dominate.

The True Story of the Morning Glory Boys

Larry Barnhill

FIRST EDITION

Manufactured in the United States of America

Paperback ISBN: 979-8-9923882-0-6
eBook ISBN: 979-8-9923882-1-3

Library of Congress Control Number: 2025900511

Copyright © 2025, Larry Barnhill

All Rights Reserved

No part of this book may be reproduced or transmitted in any form or by any means without the written permission of the publisher.

Certain names and identifying details have been changed to protect the privacy of individuals.

BnB Holdings Publishing, LLC

In association with Broader Thoughts Production, LLC

To Marion "Skip" Davis

Your interest and belief in my story gave me the encouragement and motivation I needed to continue. Your friendship gave me the strength.
None of this happens without you.
Rest in peace, my friend.

1

UPSTANDING CITIZEN

In a six-by-ten-foot cell, you have a lot of time to think about things. Like how you got there. I don't mean the standard stuff—the arrest, the hearings, the sentencing. I mean how you *got* there. How do you go from a beautiful house in a gated community to a room in a federal penitentiary? How do you go from making $100,000 a year to making $1 an hour doing prison odd jobs? How do you go from having a variety of women to a life of late-night showers with nothing but pictures on the wall?

I had a lifestyle others would envy. They shouldn't. You see, the real story isn't so much how I destroyed my lifestyle; the real story is how I let my lifestyle destroy me.

It was twenty-four years ago, but I visualize it clearly in my mind. The end—and I might as well begin there—was ugly. And inevitable.

Taylor and Bradley were the first to enter through the double glass doors that led into the lobby of the bank that day.

Cannon and I were right behind them. Mine was the last set of eyes to look behind us as we went in, making certain nobody was following or pulling into the bank's parking lot. That was my job. We each had a designated role throughout the entire process, and those roles were well rehearsed, both in practice and in previous bank jobs. We were well trained. We were a well-oiled machine.

Once in, we exploded into action, taking control of our assigned areas, which then gave us control of the bank. I remained at the door, clicking the stopwatch. We always gave ourselves one minute and ten seconds to get in and get out. Bradley covered the lobby area. Taylor directed the manager to the vault, and Cannon directed the head teller to the ATM room. Our style was what made us so damn successful; for sheer speed, of course, but also because it gave us a sense of professionalism. We weren't wild, desperate criminals. The people in the bank could tell we were smart and experienced. It made it easy for them to cooperate. They knew we were there to take care of business and get the hell out. *Nobody move and nobody gets hurt.*

In no time we had two large duffel bags full of money and another bag with four ATM canisters.

"Thirty seconds!" I called out.

"Where's the Federal Reserve money?" Taylor barked at the manager.

"In the receiving safe," she replied. "Behind the counter."

The Federal Reserve money—that's why we were there, really. That's why we'd all decided to do one more job. After this, we'd retire rich. The money was there because it was January 3, 2000, the first banking day of the new year. Banks were loaded with cash because of the Y2K scare. There was a fear that computers wouldn't understand the roll over from 1999 to 2000 since years, in programming code, had been abbreviated to two digits. Year ninety-nine would roll over to year zero-zero, and experts feared that this could potentially shut the whole financial network down. Computer techs worldwide scrambled for months leading up to January 1, 2000, to fix the problem, but nobody knew whether the fix would work. Banks were afraid that if something went wrong, there'd be a panic. So just in case, they'd made sure they had plenty of cash on hand. First Union in the Atlanta suburb of Lilburn was no different.

Taylor went behind the counter to retrieve the Federal Reserve money. Going behind the counter was a no-no. We'd never done it before. The area is visible to anyone in the drive-through lane outside. But the promise of the payoff was too great. Just one last job. We'd convinced ourselves the risk was worth it.

I glanced at the stopwatch. "Time!" I called out. But Taylor was still behind the counter and, so far, nobody had pulled up to the drive-through window. If he was quick, we'd be out of the bank in another fifteen seconds, tops.

But then it happened. A car circled through the lane. The driver pulled up to the window and saw Taylor standing there, wearing a mask. He drove off. It was incredible how fast he found a cop. Taylor headed back to the vault with the manager to get the keys for the safe behind the counter. It was only a few seconds, but that was all it took. I spotted the cop walking down a small, grassy hill on the far side of the parking lot. Through the lobby windows, he had a clear view inside. Our eyes locked and I saw him speak into his radio.

"Five-O!" I yelled. Everyone froze. The officer was walking around the building, looking into the windows to get a better handle on the situation. For a brief second, he disappeared behind a solid wall, and all four of us rushed for the front door. Pulling off our masks, Cannon and I ran to the car parked right outside the bank and dove into the back seat. Taylor and Bradley came through the door just as the cop came around the corner. Masks off, they motioned toward the bank, indicating to the officer, "That's where the bank robbers are." The officer wasn't buying it. Taylor and Bradley jumped into the car, Taylor at the wheel. He threw it into reverse, yelling for us to stay down. From the floor of the back seat, I could see him pull out his gun and point it out of the window. Then he floored it, tires squealing.

CONTROL. MOVE. DOMINATE.

What I couldn't see was that backup had arrived, a female officer who blocked our path with her patrol car. She took a position behind her open driver's-side door and pulled out her gun. I heard shots fired. Taylor rammed the car door, shoving the officer up against the car.

Taylor was a good driver. I'd had my issues with him, but I could not deny that he was the right guy behind the wheel. In no time we were driving down Lawrenceville Highway and for a moment I felt relief, as if we'd once again gotten away. We'd had close calls before, but none like this. The feeling of relief evaporated just as quickly as it had appeared when I heard the sound of sirens behind us. There'd been no time to switch vehicles, our usual procedure. I was sure that by now every cop and law enforcement agency within a hundred miles had a make on our car.

Taylor couldn't lose the pursuit cars. He ran the car into a few civilian cars in front of us, trying to create a small crash that would block the road behind us and give us some separation. He managed to nudge a van, causing it to turn right into the path of the cops, then he made a sharp right turn from the left lane, forcing the cars behind us to slam on their brakes, bringing the traffic to a halt. We were on Rockbridge Road and in the clear. Though I couldn't see a thing from the floor of the back seat, my feeling of relief returned.

Rockbridge was a long, winding road lined by tall trees on both sides. It felt safe. The goal was to make for the woods, where we could find cover. We knew we had only minutes before the helicopter—the ghetto bird in the sky, we used to call it—would find us. There would be no escape from that point.

Another gunshot. No, it couldn't be. I hadn't heard any sirens.

"Blowout!" Taylor yelled, gripping the steering wheel and trying to control the car, now down to three good tires. The car slowed to a crawl, and I heard metal on asphalt and smelled burning rubber. It felt like I was in that dream where you're trying to run but everything you do is in slow motion. I looked out of the back window and saw flashing lights approaching fast. It was time to bail. There was a main road ahead, with fast food joints and drugstores and gas stations. If we could reach it on foot, maybe we could blend in with the good people of Atlanta and the cops would drive right past us.

Then I saw flashing lights up ahead. The cops were closing in from both sides. Taylor wrestled with the steering wheel, guiding the car toward the trees, where it came to a stop against a sidewalk barrier.

"Split up!" somebody yelled. "Two and two!" Taylor and Cannon went left. Bradley and I went right. We sprinted for the thick woods. Out of the corner of my eye I saw the patrol cars closing in. I heard their sirens, then the screech of brakes and car doors flying open.

"Stop! Police!"

Stop? I was almost to the trees. Two shots rang out from behind me. These guys weren't letting us go. Did they know we were the Morning Glory Boys? They must have. The FBI had been chasing us for almost a decade. The papers quoted them as saying we robbed more banks than Bonnie and Clyde. We took a hell of a lot more money too—over three million dollars. They had to know it was us. Taking us alive would be the right thing to do, but I'm pretty sure they'd have had no second thoughts about taking us dead if they needed to.

It was no wonder that they hadn't been able to track us down. All our preplanning and training made us elusive. And none of us fit the profile. We had no criminal records. I'd never even been arrested. Outside of a traffic ticket here and there, I wasn't even in the system. The robberies happened all around Atlanta, but I was living a respectable life in Florida. I had a wife and son. I was a college graduate and a successful event promoter, and I had recently worked as assistant director of the Orange Bowl in Miami. I would not have been considered a likely bank robber by anybody's definition.

Nobody would have guessed it in a million years. Not my friends, not my mother, not even my wife.

And yet there I was, desperate to reach the trees on Rockbridge Road, shots flying around me.

I spent the next twenty-two years cursing that day. Cursing, really, my decision to even be there, to be with these men on this fucked-up journey to . . . where? Where did we think we were going? What was it we were looking for? More, I guess. We were always looking for more. Funny thing is, I'd had it all. I just didn't know it.

2

WILMINGTON

1968

Snow Hill is a town of around two thousand people near Maryland's eastern shore. It rests about a half-hour drive from the resort town of Ocean City to the northeast, and a half-hour drive from the much larger city of Salisbury to the northwest. I was born in Salisbury because it was the closest place with a decent hospital, but I'd spend the first six years of my life in a small house in Snow Hill, my grandparents' house. In addition to my mother and father, and my older brother and me, my mother's brother and two of her sisters lived there. There were nine of us. Sure, it was a little cramped, but the lack of space was offset by the love that we all felt in that home.

My grandfather, William Purnell, fought in World War I, receiving a presidential citation for his service. He was a strong-willed man who always took care of his family. To his five daughters, he was a protector. I remember following him around and sitting on his lap. I admired him, and even though I was little, his role as provider for the women in his life influenced me deeply. Later in life, I would struggle to fill that role and then have to live with the consequences of that struggle.

Granddaddy died while I lived in that house. I remember wandering into his closet after the funeral and finding a neatly folded American flag that I held tight to my chest.

My mother and grandmother, both strong women, carried on. They were the rocks of the family. With Grandaddy having left Grandma in decent financial shape, ours was a solid, middle-class household.

Outside, my cousins and I would run and hide in the endless fields of corn across from our house on Pocomoke Road, despite countless butt whippings and scoldings for doing so. The fear was that we'd get lost or get bitten by a snake. And there were other dangers. The Jim Crow segregation laws had only recently been repealed, and there was still plenty of prejudice and discrimination around. There were places where it wasn't safe to be a Black kid. Of course, as children, we understood nothing about this. We were mostly concerned about those butt whippings, but the lure of the cornfields was too strong to resist.

CONTROL. MOVE. DOMINATE.

My mother and grandmother worked long days at the Buddy Boy chicken processing plant, and one of my favorite memories is of standing on Pocomoke Road in front of our house, gazing down the road as far as I could see to watch for the car that would bring Mom and Grandma home every late afternoon. The car was full of factory workers being dropped off at their homes, and I remember the weary expressions and tired, slumped bodies. But when my mother and grandmother got out of that car and saw us waiting on them, big smiles spread over their faces. Even at that young age, I admired how hard my mother worked to keep our family moving forward. The family grew when my two sisters were born, and in 1968 we moved 120 miles north to Wilmington, Delaware.

The primary male influences in my life after my grandfather's death were my father, my uncle Buck, my uncle Sly, and my uncle Robert. Dad dabbled in his own auto detailing business and would sometimes work at an after-hours nightclub. Uncle Buck was in law enforcement. A pioneer coming out of the Jim Crow days, he was the first Black deputy in the sheriff's department. In 1972 he became the first Black correctional officer of the Worcester County Jail, and then, in 1981, the first Black person to serve as warden. Uncle Sly was also in law enforcement, serving as a police officer in New Rochelle. A member of the Masonic order, and the Grand

Basileus for the Shriners, Uncle Sly was very well respected in the community.

But it was Uncle Robert who had the most influence on me. Robert was married to my mom's sister, the only sister to graduate from college. He was a Vietnam War vet and a decent, hardworking man. He had a sense of humor that kept us laughing, and I noticed how well he treated my aunt and the other women in his life. Just like Granddaddy. Uncle Robert often took me on car rides, and as we'd drive along, he'd talk to me about being a good, strong kid. "Never quit, Larry," he'd say. "And whatever you do, you do it your best." Years later, in my second year of college, Uncle Robert was killed in a car accident. Because of scholarship obligations and financial pressures, I couldn't get away for the funeral. I carried Uncle Robert's loss all alone. But in the worst of times in college, I would always remember those car rides and the things he said to me.

Our Wilmington neighborhood was working class and racially divided. Black and Hispanic people made up parts of it; Polish and Italian people made up other parts. But all the neighborhood kids met up after school at the Jackson Street Boys Club. This is where I grew up and learned values. The club taught respect and honesty and integrity. I learned self-motivation there. We played sports, learned life skills, and were even exposed to different cultural arts. Most importantly, the club kept me off the streets.

There were terrific role models at the club, and the two biggest ones for me were Calvin Perry and Earl Christy. Earl was a former Super Bowl champion with the New York Jets, and Calvin later became head track coach at Grambling University. Both these men dedicated themselves to pushing all of us to be successful. My athletic abilities began to blossom at the club, and while Calvin and Earl encouraged my participation in sports, they pushed me in other directions too. We were all taught the importance of education, and we learned how to be well-rounded young men. Years later, after the arrest, Calvin would support me, being one of several men from my past who would decide not to abandon me.

The influences from the club helped when I reached high school. This was in the seventies, the days of forced busing. Schools had to comply with the federal order to integrate; white kids were bused to Black schools and Black kids were bused to white schools. I ended up attending Glasgow High in Newark, Delaware, way out in the suburbs. This was my first experience attending an all-white school, but my time interacting with kids of different ethnicities at the Boys Club prepared me to engage with my new classmates in a respectful way and, for the most part, I was treated the same, at least initially. It didn't hurt that I played basketball and played it well. As a freshman, I started on the junior varsity team and even played varsity a little. Everybody seemed to agree that I was a rising star, and that went a long way toward helping me fit in.

After a while, I felt comfortable at the school. Nobody seemed to like the idea of forced busing, and there were times I felt eyes on me as I walked down the hallways to class, but the resentment seemed much less than I'd figured it would be. Or maybe I hadn't been paying attention, because one afternoon, my feelings about the school changed. I was taking my seat right before science class when I felt a sudden, sharp pain in my ass. I turned to see a white kid standing right behind me. He had stabbed me with a pencil. "That seat's taken," he said, glaring at me.

As I was thinking about what to do next, the teacher came into the room and I pointed out the pencil, still partly stuck in me. "Better go to the nurse's office," he said and off I went, looking back once more at the kid who'd stabbed me, as if to let him know that he and I weren't at all finished yet. Truthfully, though, I couldn't take the chance of being kicked off the basketball team, so I decided to go through the proper channels. I explained to the nurse what had happened, and then I even explained it to the principal. I knew they would handle it. I'd been stabbed with a pencil by a kid who, apparently, was being taught to be racist. I expected the school would take care of the situation.

But the school didn't. Nothing happened to the kid who'd stuck me in the ass with a pencil, and it soon became clear to me that I had to handle the situation myself. One day in the boys' room in the recreation yard, I caught up to the kid, and let's just say I took care of my business. He never so much as looked at me again. And if he had tried anything, he knew that the other players on the basketball team, even though they were white, would've had my back.

Although the incident was over, I never felt the same about Glasgow High again. I found myself looking over my shoulder all the time. Maybe the stabbing was just a single prank, but I didn't feel like taking that chance. If there was one violent racist in the school, there were sure to be others. I talked to my mom and dad, and they agreed to transfer me to the inner-city school that my brother was attending. Howard Career Center was a predominantly Black school and provided technical and vocational trade classes. A lot of the kids were from the neighborhood, and I adjusted well. What excited me most were the school's athletic programs, tops in the state.

One student from the neighborhood, a senior by the name of Jeff Starkey, took me under his wing after I transferred to Howard. Jeff was going places. He excelled in sports and was a top student too. I'd known him from the Boys Club, where he was always a leader to the rest of us. Jeff had won all sorts of Boys Club awards, including Man of the Year. Me, I wanted to follow in his footsteps and do everything he did. Jeff helped me choose a technical trade path to follow, and I began taking architectural design classes. He talked about college a lot too, and after he graduated, he enrolled in Hampton University in Virginia. When he was home for the summer, he'd check in on me and make sure I was keeping clear of trouble and focusing on school and sports. Jeff was a great role model for me in those days.

I became a popular kid at Howard. I did well on the basketball team and became one of the top architectural drawing students. School was going well. Then, in my junior year came a bad break. Everyone seemed to think I'd do great things that year on the basketball team, and there had been a lot of anticipation.

The school hired a new basketball coach, a coach who'd been affiliated with the H. Fletcher Brown Boys Club from the east side of town, rivals to the Jackson Street Boys Club on the west side, where I had played. Most of the upcoming young players on the high school team were recruited from Brown Boys Club, but the coach knew me from those days. He knew I was good. But his relationships with the coaches at Brown were strong, and they had passed along to him their experiences—witnessing me constantly trash-talking their point guards during our fierce crosstown rivalry games. The coach soured on me. But once practice for the new season started, I figured none of the stuff from the old days mattered. I was one of the top up-and-coming players in the city, better than some of the guards from Brown Boys Club who were trying to make the team.

On the last day of cuts, I was warming up on the court when a couple of friends of mine on the team came up to me. One said, "Barnhill, you know you been cut?"

"Yeah, you real funny," I said.

"No, man, for *real*."

"What you talking about? That's bullshit."

"Check out the board, man. I'm not bullshitting."

I went into the locker room where the final cuts were listed and stood there, shocked to read my name on the board. I knew it had to be the history I had with Brown Boys Club. I was crushed, resentful, and humiliated. Basketball was my love, and I thought it was my future. For a week, I couldn't even bring myself to show up at school. When I finally did return, I kept a low profile.

Then came an opportunity. As it happens, the coach of the school track team, Bob King, had approached me before I'd been cut. He held sprints in the hallway one day and asked me to take part, matching me up against one of the top sprinters on the team. I lost by a step, but Coach King liked what he saw. But with basketball in my blood, I couldn't focus on track, and I didn't pursue the opportunity. Now that I was off the basketball team, there was nothing stopping me.

My first competition was at Weidner College. I was entered in the fifty-meter dash, and in my preliminary race I finished third, high enough to qualify for the finals but with room to be better. My teammate Kevin Marshall pulled me aside after the race and worked with me on my starting technique. His help made all the difference. In the finals I not only won—I won in record-setting time. The next day's local paper picked up on the story, declaring, "A Star is Born." My basketball career might have been over, but my track career was just beginning.

3

THE PROPOSITION

1992

Calvin Taylor was the one who got me involved.

Hell, that's not true. I could use Taylor as an excuse, but I know, especially after all this time to reflect, that I damn well got myself involved. Still, it was a lot of temptation for any man to resist.

By the early 1990s Taylor and I had already made numerous drug runs. Twice a month we'd made the ten-hour drive from Miami, where I had the cocaine connections, to Atlanta, where Taylor had an operation running out of the Harris Homes Housing Project. David Cannon was involved too. So was Edwin Bradley, my cousin, the one who'd introduced me to these guys.

Each drive was good for about $30,000, split four ways. It was fair money, and I'd been able to live like a rock star—all the coke and girls I could handle. There were endless nights drinking Moët and smoking expensive cigars in the finest strip clubs of Atlanta, doing shots of tequila with the dancers and snorting coke off their tits. All this appealed to me at the time for reasons that make no sense to me today. But it seemed perfectly reasonable to me back then.

I was between jobs too. I didn't see myself as a drug runner, even though that was exactly what I'd become. I was an unemployed white-collar event promoter and venue manager. I'd been chasing the American dream, honestly and diligently. I wasn't afraid of hard work. But the dream was snatched away from me. The company I had loyally worked for sent me to Miami, New Orleans, Memphis, and Atlanta, and I'd gone willingly each time, living out of a suitcase while setting up new arenas in those locations. These were government contracts, and it sure didn't hurt the company in the bidding process that I was a Black man. Our company could claim it was "diverse." But I was more than a token. I knew my job inside and out and I represented the company well.

Then came a management change. And the good old boys now running the organization decided a better candidate for the job would be the white guy I'd hired and trained as my second-in-command. Suddenly, my loyalty and all that I had done didn't mean a damn thing. I was out.

Temporarily, at least, I had to make other . . . arrangements. Running cocaine was not without risk, and even though the money was acceptable, Taylor had another idea that he wanted to share with me. "A better idea," he said. "More money. Less risk."

He brought it up on one of our trips back to Atlanta with bags of cocaine in the trunk. "You give me one minute and ten seconds," he said, "and I can make you ten times the money we're making on this trip."

Taylor had obviously lost his mind. "The fuck?" I said. "Man, you crazy as hell."

Turns out Taylor was serious. As it happened, and as he explained, he and Bradley and Cannon had another little venture going. "Bank robbing," he said as my jaw dropped. And they needed a fourth man.

"We took down a bunch already," he said.

"Bank robbing? Seriously? You fuckin' with me."

"Nah, man. We got a system. We got it all worked out. We're in, we're out. One minute and ten seconds. You want to keep making this fucked-up trip every couple months?"

"Yeah, but—-"

"Just hear us out. Let's head over to my place. Cannon and Bradley are there."

Cannon and Bradley just happened to be there? Clearly they'd been planning on sitting me down for a chat. A half hour later Taylor pulled into an exclusive west Atlanta suburb. We stopped in front of a mansion surrounded by a large, black iron fence.

"Who lives here?" I said.

"I live here."

"The fuck you do. I seen your house."

"Shit, man, that's my second house." Then he spoke into the intercom at the gate: "We here."

Cannon's voice answered. "C'mon in."

The gate swung open and in we drove, down a perfectly landscaped road lined by ceramic statues and finally around a circular driveway, where I saw Bradley's BMW 735i.

Inside the house I took Bradley aside. "Man, why didn't you tell me about all this, cuz?"

"Because I always felt family should be separate from business. But Taylor's insisted. Look at what you been doin' for us. Everyone here knows you can be trusted. You a real gangster, cuz. We need you."

We all sat down, and I listened for two hours as they talked to me about robbing banks. Of course the idea was crazy. It was insane. And yet I felt less and less skeptical the more I heard them talk about their operation. Honestly, I was impressed. What they'd been doing was anything but reckless. They planned each job meticulously. They practiced. They trained. And they were thinking long term.

"We hit several banks over a few days," explained Cannon, "and then we lay low."

"Yeah," said Taylor. "Two *years* low. We let time pass. We make everybody think we're gone."

"Then we come back," said Cannon.

Finally, Taylor asked the question that was on everybody's mind. "So whatchu think? You in?"

Everything they'd been saying made sense. And there was this: I knew these guys. With the drug runs, we'd committed crimes together. We were already invested in each other.

Still, I couldn't make the leap from driving around with coke in the trunk of my car to robbing a fucking bank.

"No, man, I'm sorry," I said. "Look, you all are making this shit sound easy. And I'm sure you cover your bases, but . . . but, fuck, I just can't see myself doing it. Hey, don't get me wrong. I appreciate the offer, I really do. But I'm not into this shit, you know?"

Silence followed, but soon enough Bradley was nodding and the others seemed okay too. "Cool," said Taylor.

"But listen, Larry," said Cannon, "just so you know. We out of the drug business startin' today."

Out of the drug business? But that's how I'd been making my living. As if Cannon didn't know that. Then he left the room and came back a minute later with a briefcase. He opened it up, took out a stack of fifty- and hundred-dollar bills, and handed the stack to me. Later I would count it—all $50,000 of it. The crazy thing is, that briefcase must have had ten times that amount in it.

"Take that until you make up your mind," he said.

Hadn't Cannon heard me? I'd already made up my mind. The bank robbing shit was out of the question. But this was no time to argue. I knew Cannon wasn't going to let me insult him by handing the money back. I took it.

I left the house with Bradley, my mind running a thousand miles an hour. Over a couple of beers, we talked about the offer. Bradley filled me in on other details. Like the fact that he, too, had a second home. These guys were all crazy rich.

That night I couldn't sleep. I tossed and turned, thinking about the shit they'd put in my head. But in the light of the morning, it was clear to me how fucked-up their idea was. I was no bank robber.

Over the course of the next few weeks, I continued hanging out with Bradley and Taylor. I kept expecting Taylor to propose another run to Miami, but he never mentioned it, like he'd forgotten all about the money we'd been making with the cocaine. Cannon had said, "We out of the drug business." Apparently, he was serious. They didn't need the drug money. They had the bank money. But they also knew that I had counted on the drug money and that without it, I'd piss through that fifty grand in no time. Nothing was ever said, but pulling a squeeze play on me was a clear part of their strategy. These guys weren't taking no for an answer. But they'd have to. Bank robbing? For me? No fucking way. Not in a million years. Never.

4

Fighting Gator

1980-1988

I kept winning races, and the local papers kept printing stories about me. Before long I was competing in national events like the Penn Relays, Melrose Games, and Diamond State Relays. Soon I was getting attention from everywhere. As I neared the end of my high school career, college scholarship offers began pouring in. Jeff Starkey had kindled a dream in me to attend a university, and now that dream was going to come true.

I narrowed down the choices to Tennessee, Stanford, and the University of Florida. Mainly I was looking for good architecture programs. Florida, located in Gainesville, pursued me the most diligently. An alum of the school who was a big track booster lived in Wilmington and knew of my talent and used his school connections to make sure Florida kept after me.

CONTROL. MOVE. DOMINATE.

In April of my senior year, the Florida track coach invited me down for a visit, my first trip on an airplane. It was still more or less winter in Wilmington, but when I stepped off the plane into the warm Florida sunshine, it felt like the Fourth of July. I was met by sprint coach Tommy Turner, who at one point in his lavish track career had been a member of the USA sprint team during the Black Power salute era. Some of the team members were there too, and I was given the red-carpet treatment. For an inner-city kid, this was a new experience. The weekend trip included meetings with administrators, coaches, teammates, and alumni. I was given tours of the town and campus. Everything in Gainesville revolved around the Fighting Gators. All the school's athletes stayed in Yon Hall, a private housing unit inside the football stadium with its own dining facilities. The environment and atmosphere took my breath away, and I knew right away that I wanted to be a part of the school.

Before I made my return to Delaware, I met an athletic administrator by the name of Kevin Goodman. Goodman was the only Black person working in the athletic department at the time. He was a Florida graduate and a former All-American offensive lineman. He was friendly and charismatic and made me feel even more welcome.

Later that April, back home, I entered the prestigious Penn Relays at the University of Pennsylvania. My teammates and I rode the Howard Career track team bus up from Wilmington on I-95, which happens to snake past Philadelphia International Airport. There on the tarmac we spotted a DC-10 with the University of Florida logo and the words "Fighting Gators" on the fuselage. I watched my teammates' eyes widen. Florida, aside from participating, was there to observe a lot of national high school track stars, but we all knew they were there to witness my performance as much as anybody else's.

I didn't disappoint. My performance that day in the 4 x 100 and the 4 x 400 relays had several college coaches approach me afterward. I talked to them all, but mostly out of courtesy. Deep down, my mind had been made up. I told the University of Florida coaches that I was ready to attend their school, and before they left for Florida, they held a press conference announcing my decision. My parents were there, and the proud and happy looks on their faces are what I remember most about that special day.

My college days as an athlete were everything I'd imagined they would be and more. In addition to the wonderful life on campus, being on the track team meant traveling the country to places I had never been before and meeting different people from all walks of life. I represented the University of Florida in the NCAA Track Championships in Eugene, Oregon, in 1982 through 1984. I accomplished All-SEC Track and Field three times. It was a tremendous learning experience.

All the while I got to know Kevin Goodman better. He paid attention to me and made sure I was getting along well, not just as an athlete but as a student. His mentorship led to a friendship, and after graduation he saw to it that I was offered a job as administrative assistant. Life in the athletic department was just as much fun for me as a young professional as it had been as a student athlete. Even more so. Now I was getting paid. Kevin was in charge of spring sports and facilities and the coordination of gameday skybox operations for football. I worked closely with him and met top Gator boosters. One in particular, a prominent lawyer from Miami who was on the Miami Sports and Exhibition Authority, would later help me land a position at the Miami Arena. I enjoyed my time and continued to appreciate the respect and attention people within the athletic department received. It seemed that everybody wanted to be associated with those of us on the inside.

In the late 1980s, however, I found myself receiving the wrong kind of attention. The University of Florida came under an NCAA investigation. There would be accusations of meddling by sports agents and even drug dealers. Three basketball players, one of whom I had been close friends with going back to my athletic eligibility days, would be accused of accepting money and cocaine. Eventually, the DEA would become involved. Soon enough I would find myself right in the middle of a very public scandal.

5

DEAL WITH THE DEVIL

1993

I needed the money. It was as simple as that. I'd carved out a lifestyle, but I still didn't have a job to support it. And that fifty grand was gone. Bradley came around one day to remind me about it. And to reiterate that the offer still stood.

"You know my answer," I told him.

"But the fifty stacks . . ."

"Hey, I didn't ask for that."

"But you took it. Man, they invested in you."

"Invested? Man, fuck 'em. Tell 'em go to hell."

"Cuz, you can't say that to dudes that give you fifty grand!"

We were both quiet then for a while. I wasn't going to be blackmailed into becoming a bank robber. And I didn't feel especially threatened. What were these dudes going to do, kill me? They weren't stupid. Nor did they really need the fifty grand back. Not with the money Brads told me they'd been making. Throwing the money in my face was the wrong way to get me on board. But there was another way, and Brads knew it. I couldn't keep my financial situation from him. He'd seen my lifestyle. He knew, maybe more than I did, that I needed more fuel for the fire. That was the card to play. Even still I wasn't ready. Not quite anyway.

"How much time do I have to give you an answer?" I asked Brads.

"I can buy you a week," he said, and I thought I saw just a trace of a smile cross his face. It was the closest I'd come yet to saying yes. Brads sensed my sentiments might have been changing.

"Okay," I said. "I'll let you know in a week."

It didn't take a week. I kept going over the offer in my head. The kind of money they were talking about could allow a man to live well for a long time. Really well. And there was something else that kept nagging at me. When the venue management company I'd worked for restructured and pushed me out the door, it gave me a good, clear look at how corporate America works. Sure, I'd find another position eventually, but how could I be sure it wouldn't end the same way? I needed to look out for Number One. Shit, it was just . . . well, it was just good business for me to consider Bradley's offer. I'd be stupid not to.

And this kept ringing in my head: *One minute and ten seconds.* I knew the amount of preparation these guys did. The careful professionalism they exhibited. I could do it. I could get away with it. And that was all that mattered.

I called Brads. "I'm in," I said. Then I hung up the phone and considered the thought that I might have just made a deal with the devil, maybe the biggest mistake of my life. Then the thought went away.

6

MR. MIAMI ARENA

1989-1990

The scandal at the University of Florida was difficult. I'd never before experienced the kind of public pressure I was suddenly under. It seemed as if all eyes were on me. Several athletes found themselves targets of a DEA investigation. In a sting operation an undercover agent had portrayed himself as a rich fraternity kid who loved to throw campus parties for the athletes. He provided drugs, which some of the athletes took. Meanwhile, two New York City sports agents were being accused of meddling by coming to campus and trying to sign a couple of the star basketball players. The agents argued that their solicitation of the players was legal because the players were already ineligible for NCAA play: they'd been provided money and special favors. By whom? Larry Barnhill, they said. I was the scapegoat the agents were trying to use to get themselves off the hook. They argued I'd given cash to several players and had even done drugs with them and said they had two athletes ready to testify against me.

None of it was true. But the accusations and rumors were painful, and the potential ramifications could have meant the end of my career. I had trouble eating and couldn't sleep. I wasn't the only one affected. By then I was married. I'd met Anna on campus. She was beautiful. In fact, she'd been a regular on the pageant circuit and a few years earlier had been a finalist in the Miss Teen Florida competition. I tried to shield her as best I could, but I knew the public scrutiny was just as hard on her as it was on me.

In the end, after months of investigation, I was fully exonerated. Nobody could show a connection between me and the sports agents. Nobody had any evidence that I'd paid athletes cash or given any favors. The Florida athletic department had stood behind me the whole time, for which I was grateful. Nevertheless, I became cynical and the experience soured me on college athletics.

When an opportunity came my way in 1989 to join Leisure Management International as event manager for the Miami Arena, the new multipurpose facility where the NBA Miami Heat played, I jumped at it. It wasn't as though I hadn't enjoyed my time at the University of Florida. Scandal aside, it had been a great learning experience. But I was ready for something new and exciting, and the scandal made the decision easy.

I loved Miami right away. It was a big, cosmopolitan city, fast and glamorous, with beautiful beaches and a glitzy nightlife. My new position kept me busy with major concerts and NBA games, and I met celebrities constantly. It was an exciting time for me, with what seemed like infinite potential. I became the trusted go-to person for the arena's operations department. The president and general manager of the arena took a special interest in me and took me under his wing. My experience at the University of Florida dealing with behind-the-scenes pre-production preparations for sporting events gave me a big leg up in my new job, and the president quickly had me on a fast track. He would consult with me on e-marketing and promotions for different events, and I began to sit in on post-event settlement meetings. I worked my collegiate relationships to bring rivalry basketball games and tournaments to the arena.

During this time the arena dealt with three major concert promoters: Haymon Entertainment, Cellar Door Productions, and Fantasma Productions. I built solid relationships with all three but developed personal ties to two gentlemen at Haymon—Freddie Chesson and Skip Davis. Freddie C and Skip were directly involved in the development of the major R&B and hip-hop rap concerts around the country.

CONTROL. MOVE. DOMINATE.

The Miami Arena was relatively new in dealing with major Black concerts, but Freddie C and Skip became confident in my ability to handle all the venue preparations and the artists' various rider requirements. They liked how the event settlement at the end of the night ran smoothly too.

Skip and I became close friends, and he'd become my source for entertainers for visiting VIP guests in the luxury suites. Later, as I relocated to various arenas, Skip would continue to count on me. No matter where we both were, if he needed advice or assistance with anything related to venue operations, I was the guy he'd call. If he needed me to come to where a show was or consult with him on some event problem, he knew I'd be there for him. Freddie C would relocate his residence to Atlanta, and I would spend many weekends visiting him. Both Freddie C and Skip would go on to have successful careers in the entertainment industry, but my friendships with them transcended business. These guys became like family to me.

Meanwhile, I rekindled a friendship with a young lady named Joann. I had first met her in college on road trips to Miami with my college running mate, Walter Odom, a star tight end for the Gator football team. Joann had three brothers, and I became like a fourth. One of those brothers was Bob, and everyone knew him as Bobby Dollar. Joann was tall and beautiful and exotic and reminded me of Naomi Campbell. She was very attractive to the athletes and stars I was meeting through my work at the arena, and I had her working as hostess for the VIP suites that I set up for all the concert events. She'd coordinate limos and food for the guests. I'd always stop in at the suites during the events and give out backstage passes, which the guests loved. I was becoming well known to the rich and famous who came through the arena. Joann would invite them to the exclusive local clubs too, and I'd move among them like a celebrity myself. I fit right in.

In the meantime, I became close to Bobby Dollar. Bobby was in the music industry, promoting and marketing Black concert events locally. He split his time between Miami and Tallahassee and was a high roller in both cities. We ran the streets hard whenever he came to Miami. With all our contacts, the club scene was ours for the taking, and we were all over South Beach and the high-class Miami strip clubs. I'd often visit Bobby Dollar in T-Town too, and we'd indulge in the club scene there just like we did in the Miami streets. Bobby seemed to have an endless supply of cocaine and money. I remember thinking that the music business must have been treating him well, but I didn't think too much more about it at the time.

My own star rose higher in 1990, when the arena was awarded the NBA All-Star Game. I met top media personalities and executives and elite NBA officials. It was another opportunity to rub shoulders with the rich and famous. The weekend of the game was an outstanding success by any measure, and I began to garner more attention from local media as a rising and influential African American arena-management businessman. We kept on hosting major events. We held family events like the Ringling Brothers Circus and the Ice Capades. We held conventions, sporting events, and one major concert after another. We were the biggest thing in Miami. People were calling me nonstop for tickets, and I found myself in sudden demand from some of Miami's hottest ladies. My office phone line was ringing off the hook. I had become Mr. Miami Arena.

Of course, all this time, I was married. By then my son had come along. Anna, naturally, didn't care for the hours I was keeping or the attention I was getting. Plus, she was homesick. She missed Jacksonville where she was from. Mostly she missed the attention of her mother, who had always doted on her. Anna had been the baby of the family. Jacksonville was only a forty-five-minute drive from Gainesville but was a good five hours from Miami. Anna made the decision one day to move back home with my son. "Just to finish my college degree," she told me. I never questioned her going back, but I should have seen the writing on the wall. Three months later she called from Jacksonville to tell me she wanted a divorce. She wouldn't be coming back to Miami.

I fell into a depression. I threw myself into my work, the only thing that seemed to make my life worthwhile, but even still I had trouble focusing and concentrating. Throughout all this time I had kept in touch with Kevin Goodman, my old friend and mentor from Florida, and we spoke often. I'd spend hours talking to him about the failure of my marriage and the loss of my son. He finally recommended that I speak to a psychologist, a family member he knew in the profession. I went into therapy not expecting much at all, but after a few sessions, I began to feel a little more positive. The therapist helped me see the big picture: I had to try to move on with my life and maintain the best father–son relationship I could under the circumstances.

Not long after that the Budweiser Superfest, a huge R&B event, was held at the Miami Arena. Bobby Dollar was there, and of course he knew everybody. It seemed as if every big-timer in the entertainment business was on hand. People kept stopping by our suite and of course I made the rounds, stopping by all the other suites to make sure everyone was having a good time and being properly taken care of. I was still fighting depression, and the mingling and socializing helped.

I came back into our suite at one point, and there was Dollar with a woman who looked like she'd just stepped off a modeling runway. She was small but curvaceous, dressed in a white pantsuit that highlighted her sexy figure. I moved around the room, talking with other guests, and felt her eyes on me. Finally I made my way over to Dollar. The sexy woman in the pantsuit approached and Dollar introduced her to me as "an associate and a friend." Dollar had a lot of women, but this apparently wasn't one of them. Donna was unattached.

"Where have you been all night?" Donna smiled at me as she shook my hand. "I understand you're Mr. Miami Arena."

"Well, I'm the event manager," I said modestly. We talked for a little and then I had to excuse myself to tend to my duties. "Maybe I'll see you later," I said.

"Oh, you'll see me later," she smiled. "We're both going with Bobby in his limo after the show for a night on the town. Aren't we, Bobby?"

"You know it," Bobby grinned.

"Sounds good to me," I said. On my way out of the suite, I glanced back at Dollar, who was smiling at me. He knew how down I'd been. Clearly he'd set up the meeting with Donna. Good old Bobby Dollar. You can always count on a friend.

7

BANK ROBBER

1993

Cannon opened his front door and waved me inside. "What's up, homie?"

I said, "My expectations. Let's get down to business. I ain't here on no social call."

"Relax, man. Have a beer."

I grabbed the beer he handed me and said, "If I'm going to be involved in this shit, we gonna do it right. Professional like."

Cannon looked over at Brads and sort of smiled and then turned back toward me. "Why don't you follow me down to the basement."

I couldn't believe it. Cannon's enormous basement was laid out exactly like the First Union bank, our target, all the way down to the glass entry doors, the islands where the customers filled out their deposit slips, the main counter, partitioned office cubicles with desks, and, of course, the vault.

"Shit," I said. "You built this?"

"It's an exact replica," said Cannon, and I could tell he was proud of it.

Over the course of a month, we practiced in Cannon's basement. The idea was to operate with military precision. I held the stopwatch. The whole thing had to be pulled off in under one minute and ten seconds. Little by little I found myself taking control of the training. My corporate background kicked in. This was another business operation, as far as I was concerned. And I was determined to make sure we did it fucking right. The plan was three parts and simple as pie: *Control. Move. Dominate.*

We practiced pulling our masks down and entering the bank. Of course we were armed. Cannon was ex-military, and we all had experience with guns. Cannon knew the right people, and each of us had a stolen AR-15 that he'd bought on the street. We had automatic guns in our fanny packs too, but here's the thing about our weaponry: It was all for show. The AR-15s weren't even going to be chambered. We didn't want to shoot anyone. Hell, if we got ourselves into a situation where we had to shoot, that only meant we'd done something very wrong in the planning or the execution.

Everyone had their assigned role. We rehearsed the shuffling of any potential customers to the center and gaining control. We'd move fast and sure. Brads and Taylor would head for the counter. Within thirty seconds, forty-five on the outside, we wanted to be in complete command, to dominate the environment. Intimidation was a big part of the strategy, and it wasn't just the guns—it was the fact that we *knew* what the fuck we were doing. That's what had to come across.

We practiced filling duffel bags with stacks of money, using decks of cards to stand in for the cash, hundreds of them. A few of the decks would have checkers taped to them to mimic dye packs. The duffel bags were zipped up, but not all the way. In the back seat of the getaway car, my job was to submerge the duffel into a pail of water that we'd have sitting on the back seat. If a dye pack went off, I was to grab it and toss it out the window before the pack started to send out enough smoke to interfere with the driver. We practiced this in Cannon's garage. I'd be in the back seat and the guys would toss smoke bombs through the windows while I dug for the deck of cards with the checker.

We rehearsed the getaway too. The idea was to leave the bank's parking lot and blend in with the traffic. The masks came off. We wore business attire. We made only right-hand turns, taking no chances of getting stuck in a busy intersection with a long light. We'd make our way to where the second car—the switch car—was going to be. The plan was to park the switch car the day before at a big apartment complex, no more than a minute or two away. We'd leave it in the back near the dumpsters and car wash and rear exit. This area typically butted up against some woods. And we knew nobody would go around there in the morning of a workday. Most of the residents wouldn't even be home; they'd be at work. So the idea was to drive in through the main entrance, go around to the back, jump into the switch car, and exit out the rear of the complex.

The getaway car and the switch car were both stolen. Nobody could trace them to us. Getting the cars was Cannon and Taylor's responsibility. They didn't say how they did it, and I never asked.

We surveilled the bank itself too. It was a colonial-style building in a quiet suburban setting. I had a First Union account. Three times, I put on a suit and went in and made a deposit at the same time of day we planned on robbing the place, taking note of where everyone was and what they were doing. There were typically four employees: the manager, someone we figured was a loan officer, and two tellers. We knew what kind of cars they drove, and we knew what time they showed up each morning. We even learned their names.

We cased the neighborhood, studying it for days. We learned what shops would be open at what time. We learned when the cops would make their rounds. We knew of every morning jogger and every morning dog walker. Shit, we knew when the damn paper boy made his morning deliveries.

The morning. That was the key. First thing when a bank opens is always the best time to rob it. Customer traffic is light and nobody's expecting it. That's what these guys had learned, and by the time I joined they'd already robbed six banks. They knew about the dye packs too. They knew a lot. But now they had me on board, and I was confident I could take things up a notch. I felt myself embracing the challenge. It felt like a competition to me, and I knew all about competition—from my business dealings all the way back to the track meets. I was focused. I was ready to win.

As the time neared for the robbery, I knew my life would never be the same. This was going to change me. I didn't know exactly what the change would be, but I had a sense that I was at some monumental fork in the road. It was hard to remain calm, but I kept telling myself this was just another business operation. Besides, we were trained and ready.

Or so I thought. Then came the day before the robbery. We all met at Cannon's, and I noticed Taylor wasn't there. Bradley told me the news. "Taylor's out," he said.

"What?! The fuck's wrong with Taylor?"

"He don't want to do it. But, fuck, we don't need Taylor, man. Besides, you've seen him lately. He ain't . . . focused."

I couldn't argue with that. Taylor had been partying hard, running around, doing coke. We'd all noticed. Still, we had trained with four. This was a hell of a time to pull out. I was pissed. An operation like this didn't need any surprise twists. Wasn't that what the fuck we'd been training so hard for in the first place? To make everything predictable and smooth?

"Take me to him," I said.

Cannon and I drove to Taylor's new mansion in an upscale neighborhood that was the home of world boxing champions, Grammy winners, and record producers. He saw us on his CCTV system as we pulled into the driveway, and the big metal gate slowly swung open, allowing us to pull up to the door through the circular driveway. Taylor greeted us there with a silver tray of cocaine. But he looked surprised as hell to see me.

"Come on down to the basement," he said, "where we can talk in private."

We passed his wife on the way, and I smiled a hello at her. Inside I wanted to punch Taylor in the face. Cannon was right; Taylor *was* out. If he was in, his wife wouldn't have been around. We'd all agreed that leading up to the heist, it would just be us four hanging together. Nobody in our families could see our comings and goings. Nobody could be made aware of what we were up to.

Down in the basement Taylor offered us some of his coke. We both shook our heads.

"So what's up?" Taylor said.

"What's up is I'm about to rob a fucking bank," I said. "What about you?"

"Didn't these guys tell you? Man, I got to spend time here with the wife. We're fixin' up the house and shit."

"Taylor, man, we all got obligations. We all got houses that need fixin' up. We all got other shit. But we *committed*, man."

"We'll pull it off some other time," he said. "Look, you need some money to tide you over?"

"Fuck you, man."

We left. On the drive back to Cannon's, I thought for a moment that maybe this was my chance to get out. Nobody could blame me now. The plan had changed. Without my consent. I had every right to jump ship. But then I thought about the money.

Cannon guessed what was going through my head. "Look, Larry, when we were training with four men, we trained like we were fucking eight men. We can do it with three. You know we can."

I didn't say anything for a long moment.

"C'mon," he said. "You still in, ain't you?"

"Fuck it," I said. "I'm still in."

CONTROL. MOVE. DOMINATE.

As darkness fell that night, Cannon, Bradley, and I cased the bank area one more time. Then, back in Cannon's basement, we walked through the robbery once more. By nine o'clock we were in bed, all at Cannon's house. From that point on we were incommunicado with the outside world. It was only us three, practically glued together.

We hit the sack early because it was important to be well rested. But that was just theory. How the fuck was I supposed to sleep? I tossed and turned for I don't know how long. I guess I must have eventually drifted off because the 4 a.m. alarm woke me out of a deep slumber.

We dressed. White shirts and ties under gray sweatsuits, all identical. The people in the bank needed to know we were a team.

At four thirty we were out the door. We gassed up the cars and put the switch car in place. Then we all got in the first car. Cannon was the driver. Bradley was in the passenger seat. I was in the back seat with a tub of water. We made our way to the final staging area, a Home Depot parking lot with a direct view of the bank. Brads and I got down on the floor. Cannon, sitting behind the wheel sipping on a cup of coffee, became our eyes. Starting around half past eight, the employees of the bank started showing up, each one right on time.

As nine o'clock got closer, I could feel my heart start beating faster. Once the bank opened, our window of opportunity would begin. Cannon would wait until there was nobody in the drive-through and nobody even approaching it. The drive-through was our weak link. We'd have control of everybody in the bank, but we couldn't control the drive-through. If somebody pulled up and glanced inside and saw us, we'd be fucked. But if the drive-through was clear, we could do our thing in the one minute and ten seconds we'd rehearsed and be on our way.

Once Cannon saw an opening, he'd take off for the bank and park right in front of the doors. Then Brads and I would storm the place. I was on the floor of the back seat, waiting for the moment. Waiting for Cannon to spot the opening and take off for those doors. Waiting to run into the fucking lobby with a gun and demanding the money. Me, an upstanding citizen and well-respected businessman.

My heart beat even faster. I could feel it pounding through my chest. I took a deep breath, trying to calm myself. I needed to get my shit together. We'd practiced and practiced; everything was going to be okay. We could pull it off. Fuck, we had to. It was either that or I was going to lose everything I ever had.

8

A MAN ON THE RISE

1990-1992

I hit it off with Donna, the sexy woman Bobby Dollar introduced me to at the Budweiser Superfest. After the event that night, we jumped into a stretch limo—Bobby Dollar and a girl he was with, and Donna and me—and we ended up at the Miami Nights nightclub in the trendy Carol City neighborhood of Miami, known for its Black music scene. We sat in the VIP section of the club, and I got to know Donna. We had a great night, and I started seeing her regularly after that. Donna was just what I needed as I came off the depression of the divorce.

My career was still going strong; in fact, my performance at the Miami Arena was getting the attention of the people at the corporate headquarters in Houston. Leisure Management was bidding to manage the Pontchartrain Center in

Kenner, Louisiana, a popular suburb of New Orleans, and they asked me to be a part of the presentation team.

But I was in demand. Officials from Greensboro, North Carolina, called me one day, asking if I might be interested in talking to them about joining the staff of their coliseum. After flying up to Greensboro to meet with them, I was flattered by a nice financial package they offered me to be assistant director of events. Meanwhile, our presentation in New Orleans went well, we won the bid, and Leisure Management asked me to be assistant director of the Pontchartrain Center. Now I had a choice to make. I talked it over with Donna and I talked it over with Kevin Goodman. In the end I decided to stick with Leisure Management and take the Pontchartrain Center position. I was building a solid career with Leisure Management, and I was sure my loyalty would pay off.

Donna's work and family in Miami meant that she wouldn't be joining me in New Orleans, but we talked about maintaining our relationship, telling each other we were committed for the long haul. By the time of my move, we'd been seeing each other for a year and a half. We thought we could make it work.

In New Orleans I lived like I did in Miami. I was meeting people, becoming well known, and enjoying an active nightlife. Bobby Dollar would come to town and we'd hit the clubs and party. I continued to do my job well and, once again, my performance caught the attention of HQ. After a year in New Orleans, I was asked to be a part of a transition team that Leisure was putting together to complete the construction of the new Pyramid Center in Memphis, Tennessee. The original investors had defaulted on the management contract, and the city was looking to us to complete and manage the project.

I checked into the downtown Memphis Crown Plaza anticipating a three-month stay, but Leisure Management asked me to remain as assistant director when the Pyramid Center opened. I accepted the job, proud that I was so well thought of by the company, knowing I was on a track to a vice president position as director of one of Leisure Management's bigger facilities. It was only a matter of time. My relationship with Donna continued, but looking back, I suppose it shouldn't have come as a surprise that, little by little, we were drifting apart, the geographical distance making things more and more difficult.

In Memphis I continued working hard, playing hard, and making important connections. I began meeting pillars of the local Black community, including Willie Herenton, the first Black mayor of the city. His mayoral inauguration was held at the Pyramid Center, and he was genuinely thrilled to see a Black man like me in an executive position with Leisure Management.

Willie would go on to serve five consecutive terms as mayor of Memphis, but I barely got a chance to fully acquaint myself with the city before Leisure Management tapped me for another position, this one in the Atlanta area—the Gwinnett Civic Center Arena. I'd been to Atlanta before. Bobby Dollar and I had been attending the Florida A&M–Tennessee State Football Classic that was held there each year. The Black mecca of the South beckoned to me. It was a fast, fun city like Miami, with money, a huge club scene, and no end of beautiful single women.

Of course Donna was still in the picture, but I was a young successful man, and women didn't exactly find me unappealing. Through my work at the Civic Center, my connections to the VIPs of Atlanta and to visiting celebrities enhanced my exposure to Atlanta's social scene. The *Atlanta Journal-Constitution* did a piece on me upon my arrival, which increased my social profile. I was a man on the rise, and I enjoyed the company of some of Atlanta's finest young ladies.

Naturally, Donna sensed it all. She would come for visits and witness my lifestyle. In fact, she learned of a relationship I was having with a young lady from Miami, and that ended up being the final straw. "Somewhere along the line, you're going to have to figure out what's really important to you," was one of the last things Donna said to me. Later there would be plenty of time for me to reflect on those parting words.

Meanwhile, I was living the high life in Atlanta. Making money and spending money. Hitting the clubs. Meeting people in the music and entertainment industry. Enjoying the life of a young, single man. I got to know all the road managers of all the biggest acts that came to town—Bon Jovi, LL Cool J, Guns N' Roses, all of them. I was the man they came to for whatever backstage needs they might have. Everyone came to know they could count on me, and I made myself an indispensable part of any touring company's experience at our venue. It could be stressful at times, but it was always exciting.

One night, Bobby Dollar was in town and we were drinking Dom Pérignon in the VIP section of Magic City, one of Atlanta's premier gentlemen's clubs. I was talking with "Earthquake," one of the more popular girls in the club and one of my personal favorites, when I happened to look up to see a cousin of mine whom I hadn't seen in probably a dozen years. The last I'd seen him was in Wilmington, Delaware. We'd practically grown up together, seeing each other all the time at family gatherings and also at Jackson Street Boys Club.

Our eyes met and we recognized each other immediately. He broke into a wide smile and came over and we hugged.

"Larry!" he said. "Man, it's good to see you, cuz!"

"Good to see you too!" I said. And it really was. It's always good to see family. And Edwin Bradley—Brads, I called him—was a great guy. The kind of guy who'd always help you out if you needed it. The kind of guy would never steer you wrong. The kind of guy you could count on. Yep, it sure was great to see Brads again. And when I found out he was living in Atlanta, that was even better. Brads and I were going to have some great times together, that much was certain.

9

CRIMINAL, OFFICIALLY

1993

Maybe I should have taken it as a sign. The drive-through lane never seemed to clear that morning. It was one car after another. The lobby had more customers than normal too. All the planning in the world can't help when circumstances turn murky.

"Fuck it," Cannon finally said from the front seat. "We'll try again tomorrow."

I was jacked up. I'd psyched myself into robbing a bank like I was getting ready to run an Olympic track event. Now I had to come down. Part of me wanted to argue; part of me wanted to say, "Come on, we can *do* this. Fuck the people in the drive-through. We'll be in and out so fast, it won't matter." But I knew the decision was the right one. A big part of the success that these guys had enjoyed came from not taking unnecessary chances and not making emotional, rash decisions. After all, using discretion and common sense was part of the planning process too.

We drove back to Cannon's house, changed clothes, and went out for breakfast. Cannon and Brads talked about everything except what had happened that morning. I could see that that was also part of their success. They could turn it on and off. I still felt the adrenaline. I didn't show it, but my heart didn't stop racing until midway through breakfast. For Cannon and Bradley, this had been another day at the office.

We fucked around the rest of the day; then, later that evening, things got serious again. The mood changed. We had a job to do the next morning. We turned in early again, and this time I slept better. When morning came, I noticed the butterflies were gone. The previous day's attempt had acted like a dress rehearsal for me. Now I felt more ready, more excited than nervous. More focused.

At nine we were back at the Home Depot, and I was back in my position, crouched down in the back seat of the getaway vehicle. Cannon was watching the drive-through. At nine fifteen he made the determination that we had the window we needed.

"Here we go," he said, and he drove for the bank, parking right in front of the doors as planned. At the same time, a couple was getting out of their car in the parking lot and heading in.

"Sit tight," I heard Cannon say from the front seat. "Black couple going in. We'll come in right behind them."

He waited until they were just about at the door, then said the magic words: *Control. Move. Dominate!*

I hit the stopwatch and we slid out of the car and swept in behind the couple, using them as shields. We pulled our masks down over our faces, and as the door opened I pushed the couple inside from behind, steering them to the middle of the lobby. "Get down on the floor," I ordered sternly but quietly. There was to be no yelling, no raised voices. We didn't want to panic the employees or customers, and we didn't want to sound jumpy or high-strung ourselves. We weren't desperate, crazed crackheads. We were professionals there to do a job and get out. The name of the game was control—of ourselves, of our emotions, and of the environment.

Bradley went left and I went right. The first priority was to handle the employees, anyone who could press a silent-alarm button. Brads slipped by a couple of small offices, waving the loan officer out from behind his desk and to the center of the room. Cannon jumped quietly over the counter and directed the teller to take a step back. He motioned for the drive-through teller to do the same, but we were all careful to remain unseen from the drive-through window. There were only three other customers in the place, and I directed them to the middle of the room. All this was done mostly by pointing. The AR-15s we had strapped on our backs said everything we needed to say.

In no time, the bank was ours.

Cannon turned to the manager and calmly said, "Cathy, give me the vault key." Knowing the names of the staff added to the image we needed to portray: we'd done our homework.

Cathy hesitated and then replied, "I . . . I don't have it."

"Liar," Cannon said flatly.

"No, really, I don't have it."

"Cathy?"

Time was wasting. I looked at the watch. "Forty-five seconds," I called out. The manager's delay left us only twenty-five seconds. There was no time for the vault. Cannon and Bradley took the money from the counter and drive-through, with Bradley ordering the tellers to pull out the dye packs. In the meantime, the manager changed her mind, deciding that she wasn't going to take any chances. She sure as hell didn't owe the bank her life.

"Here," she said, handing the vault key to Cannon. "I guess I did have it." But it was too late. I looked at the stopwatch: 1:10.

"We're out," I said.

We raced outside and into the car. Cannon took off as I put the duffel bag into the bucket of water. The tellers had taken any dye packs out like we'd asked them to, but you can never be sure. We headed to the apartment complex where we had parked the switch car, and I noticed that nobody was following us. We changed cars and headed for my SUV, switched again, and then made it to Cannon's house. I couldn't imagine that it could have gone any smoother. Part of me was elated. But there was another part. I was hit by the thought that I was now—officially—a criminal, a fugitive from the law.

Cannon took the money, put it into a pillowcase, and threw it in the clothes dryer. When it was sufficiently dry, we counted it out and split it into thirds. My heart sank. Each take was only $20,000. I'd risked my life for twenty grand?

Then I felt my anger rise. This is what these guys had dragged me into? This is why we'd practiced so hard and made such detailed preparations? Fuck, Cannon had built a replica of the bank in his fucking basement! For twenty grand?

"Fuck this," I said. "I'm out of here."

"Cuz," Brads said, "it'll get better. Sometimes this is the way it goes."

"Yeah, well, I got better prospects than this. Maybe you guys need to do this shit, but I don't." I took my money and started walking toward the door.

"Barnhill, wait." Cannon handed me half his take. "There. Maybe that'll help. Man, look, this is long-term shit. Stick with us. We'll try again and the next time will be better. A *lot* better. You just gotta hang in there, man. You see my house, right? You think all this came from one hit?"

"I'll think about it," I said, taking his ten grand.

I left Cannon's house and drove home. Telling Cannon and Bradley that I'd think about it was just something I said to get out of Cannon's house. Or was it? The truth was, the take from the bank was disappointing, but it had only been a one-minute, ten-second operation. And it had gone unbelievably smoothly. We'd gotten away with it so easily. And there was something else: I'd told the two of them that I had better prospects, but did I? It had been months since I'd lost my position with Leisure Management. The corporate world wasn't giving me shit. Maybe I was destined to be a bank robber, after all.

10

Choices

1992-1993

Brads and I partied hard. It was great having family in Atlanta. And he had some good friends, too, that he introduced me to—a couple of guys in particular by the names of David Cannon and Calvin Taylor whom we partied with often. They seemed to me like a couple of dudes living the high life, always with plenty of money. I wondered at times what they did for a living, but we never got around to talking about our work. Not back in those days anyway.

Leisure Management, meanwhile, continued to be a thriving company. But the growth ultimately led to some changes and corporate restructuring. The president and CEO left to take a position with an arena management company in the UK. Now different people were in charge. The new president felt as if he had to put his own mark on the company. Among other things, this meant I ended up reporting to a guy I had trained and who used to work for me. He was a good ol' boy from Louisiana, and it was pretty clear to me that the only reason he leapfrogged me was because the new leadership preferred one of their own kind. I'd faced racism before, but this was the first time it had directly affected my career. Worse, the move was made with a larger intent: The new leadership wanted me out. I was part of the old team, and I didn't have a place with the new one. The best I could do was negotiate a severance package. I carried a chip on my shoulder from that point on.

For anyone else the severance package would have lasted months. Me, I had no plans to surrender the high life just because I was between jobs, and it didn't matter that I had no luck finding something to replace the position I'd been pushed out of. So when the money started running out, I needed to do something about it. Cutting back on my lifestyle wasn't an option.

As it happened, I had learned that Bradley and his friends Taylor and Cannon were pretty well connected with drug dealers in and around the Atlanta area, especially at the Harris Homes Public Housing projects. At the time, I assumed that might have been where a decent percentage of their money had come from. And back when I was Mr. Miami Arena I had made my own contacts. I was a social user of cocaine, and I knew the people who knew the people.

It didn't take long for me to put the idea together of buying cocaine in Miami and running it up to Atlanta. Taylor and Cannon were on board immediately. They could use a source, and that source would be me. They never knew who I was buying it from, and I never knew who they were selling it to. I only knew that a run from Miami to Atlanta would mean a profit for all of us of about $30,000 that we'd split.

Here's what I didn't know at the time: Taylor, Cannon, and Brads didn't need the money. In fact, they didn't need to be in the drug business at all. They had another business going, but they needed a fourth person to take that business up to the level where they wanted it to go. Me running drugs was never the goal for them. Me running drugs was a way for them to audition me, to see how I operated under pressure. To see what I'd be willing to do for money. To see how many laws I was willing to break. I didn't know it, but I was the leading candidate for a new position that had opened up in an organization known as the Morning Glory Boys.

Taylor and I made the runs. We'd leave the Miami area at the very start of morning rush hour, dressed in suits like a couple of businessmen on the way to a staff meeting or a sales call. The only difference was that we'd have a kilo or two of cocaine sitting in the trunk of my car. Twelve hours later we'd deliver our cargo to Brads and Cannon.

Taylor and I made two trips a month and became close. You can't spend that much time in a car with someone without getting to know them. Of course I didn't know everything about Taylor, but soon I'd learn more than I could have imagined. On one trip to Atlanta, I was complaining about the long drives and the risk.

And that's when it happened: the proposition. The deal with the devil.

That's when Taylor calculated that I was ready. That's when he said he could make me ten times more money in one minute and ten seconds than what we were making on the drug runs. We went to his house when we arrived in Atlanta—his other house, the mansion I hadn't known about—with Brads and Cannon there to make the pitch. That's also the day that Cannon told me the drug business was ending. He asked me to think seriously about robbing banks and gave me $50,000, saying, "Take that until you make up your mind."

I should have known that he'd come to collect it eventually. And with what I'd learned about the tentative nature of career positions in corporate America, and—let's be honest—the life I wasn't willing to give up, I was left with little choice.

CONTROL. MOVE. DOMINATE.

No, that's not true. You always have a choice. In any situation, there's a right choice and a wrong one.

I swear to God, as I sit here today, I can't for the life of me figure out how in the fuck I could have chosen so badly.

11

ORANGE BOWL

Fate intervened. As I was mulling a career in bank robbing, my old friend and mentor Kevin Goodman called. He was assuming the position of executive director of the Orange Bowl Committee in Miami, and he wanted me for assistant executive director. The job paid $80,000 a year. I was ecstatic. I was back in business. Real business. Legitimate business. I could leave behind the street life and the thoughts about knocking off banks and get back to where I belonged. I could get back to chasing the career I'd had since my graduation from the University of Florida.

I moved to Miami and threw myself into my new position. Kevin and I were the first African Americans to oversee the Orange Bowl Committee in its sixty-year history. Our profile in the community was high. I found myself working closely with local and state government officials, and soon I was serving on boards and interacting with various businesses throughout the city. As that first December neared with the Orange Bowl game just a month away, things went into overdrive. I spent most of my time entertaining sponsors and other VIPs. I was legit partying again and life was good.

I kept in touch with Bradley—family is family—and even invited him down to the Orange Bowl that year. Nothing was ever said about my previous life in Atlanta. We just had a good time at the clubs. He came down the next year too. Again, neither of us really said anything about the old days. Bradley never mentioned Taylor and Cannon or robbing banks, and I sure as hell wasn't going to ask. All that was in my past.

The next year rolled along with me on top of the corporate world. Then things got even better. Bobby Dollar's brother introduced me to a woman named Regina. Regina was a graduate of Spellman College and a high school counselor for Dade County Public Schools. I invited her to lunch. She met me in my office in downtown Miami and then we jumped into my four-door Mercedes. But we didn't get beyond the parking lot. I rolled down my window to compensate for the broken air conditioning and she said, "Oh, no. Uh-uh. No way am I riding in a car without air conditioning. I'll drive." So much for impressing Regina. It's funny. With another woman, I might have been embarrassed or pissed off. But I could tell by Regina's reaction that she was a strong-willed person, and I liked that. Plus, she was good natured about it.

We had lunch that day, and before long we were seeing each other all the time.

Regina came along at the right time. I was ready for a serious relationship. Up until then I'd had casual girlfriends. Lots of them. I'd hooked up with girls I'd met in the course of my work, and I'd hooked up with girls I'd partied with at the strip clubs. But Regina was the type of woman a man could settle down with for good. We dated for about a year and then I asked her to be my wife.

Regina and I had the kind of wedding every girl dreams of. We had family and guests come from all over, and I put them all up at the Eden Roc Resort Hotel overlooking the Atlantic Ocean, all expenses paid. We had pre-parties and pre-dinners. One memorable moment was at a United Negro College Fund event hosted by the Orange Bowl Committee. Jazz recording artist Najee was on the stage, and at one point he said, "I'm dedicating this next set to Larry and Regina who are about to be joined in marriage. I wish you two the very best." Then he launched into Anita Baker's "Sweet Love." Regina put her head on my shoulder, and I thought about how damn lucky I was.

Our wedding was the social event of the season. After our honeymoon in Hawaii, we moved into our first house, in an upscale neighborhood with gated security. My life was now perfect. Or so I thought.

I invited Brads down again for the Orange Bowl that year, and Regina was cool with letting us cousins go out and paint the town together. Sure, I was married, but I wasn't dead. I hadn't stopped my partying ways. What's a little coke here and there and some high times at Miami's finest gentlemen's clubs?

The night before the big game, Bradley and I were out in my Lexus 400 Coupe. The Mercedes with the broken AC was a memory by that time. Conversation ranged all over the place, but I sensed Bradley had something on his mind. Sure enough, he turned to me at one point and said, "Larry, we got it all set up, man. We need you, big guy."

"Got what set up? What you talkin' 'bout?"

As if I didn't know. Then he explained it. Three banks, one week.

"Forget about that shit," I told him. "I got me a *life* now. I got a beautiful wife, a new house, a great career. I ain't about to give all that up."

"Yeah, but cuz, don't you see? That's what makes it so perfect. You can come to Atlanta and rob a bank behind a mask and ain't nobody *ever* gonna track you down, let alone suspect it's you behind that mask."

He said it again a couple of days later as I drove him to the airport, but he put it like this: "The name of the game is to be able to exist in an environment that only you can observe, while being seen in a completely different way. That's what can make this work."

I thought a lot about that over the next few days. The name of the game was to live a double life. That was the secret to their success.

Things at the Orange Bowl were going great. As assistant executive director, I was responsible for overall daily administration of the Orange Bowl Committee office and for the development of relationships with local government officials. I was also responsible for the management of the game, the Orange Bowl parade, and a multitude of other related events. I worked to bring in revenue and I knew my business well. Through merchandising, licensing, and the addition of national sponsors, I was able to make millions for the committee. I was paid well too.

But my expenses were high. Regina and I lived in an upscale neighborhood. I drove a luxury car and wore expensive suits. And then, of course, there was the partying. "Entertaining sponsors and other VIPs," I would tell Regina. "You know, networking. Making important contacts." Some nights that was the truth. Most nights it wasn't. Most nights it was Moët and premium cigars in the best gentlemen's clubs Miami had to offer. And they had *a lot* to offer. I threw money at the dancers as if I had an unlimited supply of it. I'm sure that somewhere in the back of my mind I must have known my lifestyle was unsustainable, but on those nights in Miami I was living anywhere but in the back of my mind.

Fuck, I already had a double life going. What was one more? Brads's words kept echoing in my head. *Exist in an environment that only you can observe, while being seen in a completely different way.* I called him a week after he left. "I'm in," I said.

12

ONE WEEK, THREE BANKS

Somewhere in the air between Miami and Atlanta, the disturbing thought occurred to me that I was somehow being reborn into a bank robber, like I was being hatched from some really fucked-up egg. But then I thought, *No, that's not me. I'm a corporate player. I'm a white-collar executive.* That one heist at the First Union? That was a million years ago, and you could hardly call it a robbery. We didn't make shit. And these three banks were going to represent the end of any illicit activity on my part. I was just going to make a little money to maintain my Miami lifestyle. Nothing more. Taylor and Cannon and Bradley might have been bank robbers, but I was different. I was a businessman.

As far as Regina knew, the trip was all business. I had Orange Bowl obligations in Atlanta, and it was perfectly reasonable that I'd be flying up there. "There's a lot of bonus dollars in it," I'd tell her. In fact, one trip turned into several. Say what you want about the gang I was about to join, but these dudes didn't do things half-assed. The whole operation was based on being ready. We were going to take a month and prepare for robbing these three banks like we were getting ready to play the fucking Super Bowl.

For a month, I would fly back and forth between Miami and Atlanta, telling Regina, "It'll all be worth it, babe, you'll see." I don't know to this day what she thought of the trips, but I know she liked the money and the lifestyle we'd built, and maybe that's why she never asked a lot of questions. Only thing is, I needed to meet her expectations.

The first of the three banks we planned to rob was another First Union, and the scheduled date was the first business day of the new year—1995. This time Taylor was with us. Four men made everything a lot more efficient than three, and I appreciated Taylor's presence. But I was still pissed off that he hadn't been with us for the '93 robbery.

We practiced as before, but now, with a fourth man, we changed the roles slightly. Taylor would go for the vault, Cannon would hit the ATM. Brads and I would take control of the employees and customers, with me also keeping an eye on the stopwatch.

At 9:15 a.m., we struck with our well-rehearsed military precision. In fifteen seconds the bank was ours. This time the manager immediately handed the vault keys to Taylor, who, like Cannon in the previous job, called her out by name. Cannon had the ATM machine opened from the back, and he slid out the four currency boxes, dumping the money cannisters into his duffel bag. We knew the ATMs were always lucrative, especially in these neighborhoods. These were well-to-do areas, and the banks had to make sure the machines were filled. Sometimes there was as much as $100,000 to $150,000 in them. And you didn't have to worry about dye packs.

From inside the vault, I heard Taylor call for more bags after he'd already filled two. We didn't have any more. "Garbage bags!" he said. "Anything to put money in."

By then, however, we were forty-five seconds into the job. "Forty-five!" I called out. But Taylor wasn't coming out of the vault. Cannon and I exchanged glances, and I knew what he was thinking. The same thing I was thinking: greed was going to get us all put away.

"Five-O!" Cannon yelled out. "Now, T!" The code for police had its intended effect. Taylor shot out of the vault like a bullet.

All four of us flew out of the bank, but before we hit the doors, we noticed the phones lighting up. Someone had pressed the silent alarm, and the cops were no doubt calling to confirm it wasn't a false alarm. We piled into the getaway car and sped out of the parking lot. Taylor was driving and he was livid.

"What the fuck you callin' me out the vault for?! Shit, ten more seconds and we coulda stuffed two more bags!"

"Someone pressed the alarm, dumbass," Cannon shot back. "You seen the phones lighting up."

"Yeah, but you didn't know that when you called 'five-O'!"

Cannon looked stupefied. "What the fuck's the difference?! The cops is comin', ain't they? Maybe you'd rather still be in the fuckin' vault!"

Cannon was right. The cops *were* coming. As we made it out to the main road, we could hear the sirens.

"And why you yell out 'T'?" Taylor continued. "Man, we can't be calling out names like that."

"It ain't a name, it's a letter. Watchoo think the cops gonna do? Start arresting everyone whose name starts with a fuckin' T?"

"Fuck, man."

We slipped into the apartment complex parking lot where the switch car was but decided to go right past it. Taylor slowed down just enough to let Bradley jump out and get in the switch while we exited the rear of the complex. Bradley's job now was to follow us and make sure nobody came between the two cars.

As police cars headed for the bank, one came our direction, following a few cars behind us. Cannon and I were crouched down and Taylor was the only visible occupant. Two blocks down the street, we came to a red light and the cop pulled into the lane beside ours, coming up even with us. Bradley was still right behind us. While we waited for the light to change, the cop glanced over, but all he saw was a lone Black man in a dress shirt and tie sitting behind the wheel of an ordinary car. When the light changed, the cop turned left. We went right, and I started breathing again.

Back at Cannon's house, we counted up the take: $800,000.

Later I'd allow myself to feel happy about it, but I was still rattled from the close call. And that's why I had no patience for Taylor, who was still pissed about leaving the vault early and who, to my complete disbelief, started talking about how he was owed something from the last job—the job he was AWOL from.

"Are you fucking serious?!" I said. "Why the fuck should you get anything from *that* job?"

"Hey, we part of the same gang," he said. "We split everything."

"Not when you're not fuckin' *there!*"

"Fuck you, Barnhill. You lucky we even asked your ass to join."

That was about all I could take. I slipped my .45 out and held it up, not pointing it at him exactly, but letting him see it. "You get nothing from that job," I seethed. "You understand?"

"Cuz," Bradley said, stepping between us, "man, calm down. Look, there be plenty of banks and plenty of money for all of us."

"Maybe so, but he gets nothing from the last job."

Cannon turned to Taylor. "B-hill's right, man. Besides, we each made $200,000 today. Fuck, we should be celebratin'."

Nothing more was said about Taylor's demand or my pulling a gun, but my relationship with Taylor wouldn't be the same from that point on. Nevertheless, we both knew that we had to work together as a team. But there's no law that says teammates have to like each other.

As it turned out, there wasn't a lot of time to second-guess the dynamics of the group. Our next job was the following morning—a bank in Marietta. By then the routine had been perfected. Taylor hit the vault, Cannon hit the ATM, Bradley took care of the office staff, and I ushered the customers to the middle and watched both the door and the stopwatch.

Everything was as smooth as ice cream on a hot summer day. Except it was early January, and suddenly things weren't so smooth. I was about to call out "Forty-five" when I glanced outside to see a Loomis armored truck pulling in, blocking our getaway car. I motioned to Bradley and Cannon, who took ambush positions on opposite sides of the entrance doors. The delivery driver came in holding a bag of money, completely unaware of what was going down. In two seconds, it was him, going down to the floor, invited there by the sight of Bradley's and Cannon's guns. I grabbed the bag, an unexpected bonus.

But we still had a problem. The truck driver. When we came out, he knew something was up and immediately tried to block our exit with the Loomis truck. We piled in the car, Taylor jumped the curb, and we were gone. This time there was nobody following us. We switched cars and then drove to my SUV. Cannon took the wheel while I sat in the back seat taking inventory of our stuff—masks, gloves, clothing, and guns. Everybody's fanny pack had been handed to me. It was part of the routine; everything needed to be accounted for. Except this time something was missing. Halfway home, I discovered Cannon's gun was not in his fanny pack.

"Cannon," I said, "where the fuck your gun?!"

A look of dread came over his face. "Oh shit," he said. "I think I left it in the getaway car."

"Damn!" I said. "What the fuck?"

"We gotta go get it," said Bradley.

"Drop me off here," I said to Cannon. "Taylor, you and me will catch a cab and take this shit home. Cannon, you and Brads go back to the car and get that fucking gun."

Taylor and I were counting the money when Cannon and Brads finally made it back to Cannon's house.

"Get it?" I asked, but I could tell from their expressions that something was wrong.

"The FBI's got it," said Brads.

"Say *what*?"

"They were all over the car," Cannon sheepishly added. "Dusting for prints and shit." This probably should not have come as a total surprise. By then the FBI knew our MO. When a bank was hit by the Morning Glory Boys—the name everyone was calling us by then—the FBI knew to go to the rear of the nearest apartment complex. That's where they were sure to find the abandoned getaway car, the only car in the area with a tub of water on the back seat. Not that discovering the car would do them much good.

"They won't find anything besides the gun," said Taylor. And he was right. We wore gloves. There were no prints. And even if there had been, we weren't in the system. That was part of the beauty of the operation. They'd be looking for criminals. We were all upstanding citizens, at least as far as they knew.

"Yeah, but the gun might be enough," said Brads. "They can trace it to the dealer." Cannon's gun had been purchased from a gun dealer that happened to be a friend of Bradley's, a friend who never asked questions. Yusuf was a Muslim, and he had no love for law enforcement. He and his fellow Muslim brothers controlled the West End of Atlanta, running small merchant shops. They were continually harassed by the police, branded as potential terrorists and surveilled, just because they were of Middle Eastern descent.

"Then we better get to Yusuf before the FBI does," I said.

Brads and I jumped into my car and headed for Yusuf's place. We didn't arrive empty-handed. Brads explained to Yusuf that the Feds would be coming around asking questions about the gun.

"But you don't know anything about it," Brads said. "Right?" Then we handed Yusuf a paper bag with about $25,000 in it.

"I understand," Yusuf said, taking the bag. "I'll take care of it."

Yusuf would later be questioned by two FBI agents. As it happened, the guns Yusuf sold to us were guns he himself had reported stolen soon after he'd received them. So there were police records showing the theft. Of course they hadn't really been stolen. Yusuf had just set some guns aside for people like us and told the cops they'd been taken. When the FBI showed up, he reiterated his story and showed the agents the original police report. And that was the end of that lead.

We pulled off one more job that week as scheduled. Everything ran smoothly, and we allowed ourselves to celebrate that night, hitting the Magic City gentlemen's club. And that's where another lead reared its ugly head. The drinks were flowing, the music was loud, and the girls were hot. We were all having a great time when another patron started to make small talk with us. He was all smiles and seemed like he was enjoying himself at the club, and then he came out with, "Hey, ain't one of you guys 'T'?"

We should have known. Witnesses at the First Union bank no doubt reported that four men were the perpetrators, and one of them was referred to as "T." In the minds of the FBI, that probably meant four street thugs who would blow all their money at one of Atlanta's premier hot spots. Magic City was a likely place, so they came in undercover and started looking for guys spending a *lot* of money. Sure, that was us. But we were no street thugs. The people at Magic City that night weren't in our circle. Nobody there knew us, and surely nobody would know one of us as "T." In the FBI's defense, their assumption made more sense later when we learned that they'd picked up a dye pack near the Harris Homes Housing Project. I'd tossed it out the window as we'd happened to be driving by on our escape route the morning of that job. They figured Harris Homes is where we operated from. How could they have known we all lived in exclusive neighborhoods in expensive homes?

After the smiling undercover guy asked if one of us was T, we all just shook our heads and went about our evening. Then, one by one, taking our sweet time, we each drifted off and got the fuck out of Magic City.

In truth, the FBI was at a total loss. I began my drive back to Miami the next morning to resume my life as an honest businessman, but in Atlanta, every television news program led off their broadcast with the news that the Morning Glory Boys had struck again. Three times in one week. FBI Special Agent Jeff Holmes gave a press conference, but Holmes didn't have much to say. A tall white man with silver hair and a serious expression that conveyed his twenty-plus years with the bureau, he seemed legitimately stumped. And frustrated. Why wouldn't he be? He'd been chasing the Morning Glory Boys even before I had come aboard. The three heists that week represented numbers eight, nine, and ten for the gang. Ten banks robbed, no decent leads. All Holmes could do was wait for us to make a mistake.

On my drive back to Florida, I thought I was going to be the one to make it. An hour outside of Atlanta, I was pulled over for crossing the center line. I took a deep breath as the police officer came up to the driver's side window. I was dressed, as usual, in a suit. I had my briefcase open in the passenger seat with legal pads and business papers clearly visible. To complete the disguise, I was talking into my phone as I rolled the window down.

"Thanks, Sheila," I was saying. "Just tell him we'll go over the proposal tomorrow at the board meeting. Gotta go." I hung up, turned to the cop, and smiled. "Good morning, officer. Can I help you?"

Then I tried like hell to put it out of my mind that I had a duffel bag in the trunk that contained $300,000 of stolen bank money.

13

Money, Money, Money

The cop and I exchanged a few pleasantries, then he told me he had pulled me over for crossing the center line.

"Sorry, officer," I smiled. "I should have been paying closer attention. You had every right to pull me over."

Maybe if I had been white, he would have let me go right then, possibly with a citation at worst. But I wasn't white. And even though I was dressed in business attire, he still felt the need to ask the following question: "Do you have any illegal guns or substances in your vehicle, sir?"

Now, I could have just said no, but I knew the odds. During routine traffic stops, people of color are twice as likely to have their cars searched as white people. It was best to cooperate, to play the honest citizen, to give the officer something. Anything to keep him out of the damn trunk.

"No, sir," I replied, "but I do have a registered gun in my glove box."

"I see. Well, I'm going to have to call it in and check it out. Then I'll have you on your way. If I could get you to step out of the vehicle, please."

"Of course, officer."

I got out of the car and the cop walked me over to the grassy rise at the side of the road and told me to stand there. Then he opened the passenger side door, reached into the glove box, grabbed the gun, and walked back to his car, where he called in the registration number. Several minutes went by, and then a second police car came upon the scene and pulled in behind the first. Coincidence? Or had the first officer called for backup? I felt my pulse quicken. The gun was perfectly legal, and there was no reason for any suspicions on the part of the cops, but a duffel bag full of stolen cash in your trunk can make a man nervous. That, of course, was the one thing I couldn't show.

The second cop had a word or two with the first and then sauntered over to me. "Good morning, officer," I smiled.

"Sorry about the delay," he said, "the computers are a little slow."

"Sure, no problem."

Then he asked me what I did for a living, and the next thing I knew, we were chatting like old friends.

Eventually, the first cop stepped out of his car and came over to me, handing me the gun with the empty clip and bullets in a plastic bag. "Okay, Mr. Barnhill, you're free to go. We kept you here a little longer than I'd planned, so I'm not going to give you a ticket, but promise me that if you absolutely have to talk on the phone, you'll pull over to a rest area to make the call from now on, okay?"

"I sure will, officer. Thanks."

"Have a great day."

I got back in the car and went on my way, taking a few deep breaths to calm myself. I felt a sort of pride that I'd been able to maintain such composure. But just like the proverbial duck on the pond, gracefully sliding across the water, I'd been paddling like hell underneath.

I drove on, but now I couldn't stop looking in my rearview mirror. I was certain I was going to get pulled over again, and the next time, they'd surely search the trunk. By the time I'd reached Jacksonville, my nerves were shot. I'd planned to spend a few hours there anyway, to be with my son, so it was a good time and place to regroup, but I decided it was also a good place for me to stop fucking driving. I called Kayleigh, a friend of mine from Fort Lauderdale who was a flight attendant.

Kayleigh was an attractive young lady, born and raised in Jamaica. I'd met her one day at a Cellular One store. We'd talked briefly about general life stuff, and later that day the store manager, a University of Florida graduate, called to tell me that Kayleigh had asked for my number. Pass it on, I told him. Not long after that Kayleigh and I were frequently talking by phone. She came from a strongly connected family but was mourning the recent loss of her husband. Over time we became close friends.

"Take the next flight here," I told Kayleigh after I'd reached Jacksonville, "and I'll give you five grand to drive me to Miami."

By the time I was done having lunch with my son and doing some shopping with him and his mother, Kayleigh had arrived. I picked her up at the airport and told her to get behind the wheel.

"Larry," she said, "what kind of trouble you in?"

"Aww, I ain't in no trouble," I said. "Just need a little company is all."

"You transportin' drugs, aren't you? Larry, why you doin' shit that's gonna fuck up your life?"

"Honest, I ain't transportin' no drugs." Of course Kayleigh didn't need to know any more than that. She didn't need to know what was in the trunk.

On the way to Miami, I called the Hilton in Fort Lauderdale and reserved a top-floor suite. I knew I needed to decompress for a night before going home to Regina. And I needed to stay somewhere safe.

At the Hilton, I checked into my suite and Kayleigh and I had dinner and drinks in the downstairs restaurant. I slipped her the five grand, and she said, "What you gonna do with that big suite all by yourself?"

"Rest," I said.

"C'mon, Larry. You know I know your ass. If you wanted to rest, you would have taken your ass home. So call Rachel and Kenny and let's get the party started."

The truth was, I could use a party. I needed to unwind, and it might be fun to throw a little blowout. But I needed to take care of something first. I excused myself from dinner to "make a private call" and made my way to the front desk. I'd noticed when I'd checked in that my suite adjoined another room, and I asked if it was occupied. By good fortune, it wasn't.

"I'd like to take that room too," I told the desk clerk.

Five minutes later I had retrieved the duffel from the car and locked it securely in the adjoining room. Now I had a room for the party and a separate room for the money. I called Rachel, a longtime friend who I liked to party with, my ride-or-die chick. "Bring some friends, baby," I told her, and she knew what I meant. Kenny was a loyal friend and bodyguard with a solid street reputation, and I called him too.

An hour or so later the party started. Rachel showed up with three of her stripper friends from Club Rolexx. I ordered food and drinks, and soon the music was playing, the lights were low, and it was as if Kenny and I had our own private strip club. Soon the cocaine made its appearance. Meanwhile, I was throwing money at the dancers like, well, like I'd just robbed a bank.

I knew the girls from the club, all except for one. Tiana was sexy as hell, but quiet. At one point she sat down with me and we started talking. "I'm just dancing at Rolexx until I can find a full-time job," she told me. "Do you have one for me?"

"What makes you think I'd have a full-time job for you?"

"You a successful businessman, ain't you? I can tell this environment here isn't you. You're just doing this to impress your friends, playing the part because you have money."

Nobody had ever read me that quickly. What had she seen or sensed about me? Her words would stick with me for days, mostly, I suppose, because on some level I knew she was right. I wasn't really that guy, the guy partying and doing coke and throwing money at strippers and living in hotel suites. But that's what success looks like, isn't it? Isn't that what you do? Wasn't that why I was so intent on hauling in as much money as I could, by whatever means necessary?

The party broke up eventually, and Kenny took the girls home. Tiana stayed with me for the night, but we didn't sleep together. We just talked until the wee hours before finally falling asleep. In the morning I called room service for breakfast, then checked out and drove Tiana home to a duplex she shared with two friends and her son. She gave me her cell number, and I promised I'd call, a promise I knew I'd be keeping. This was a woman I wanted to see again.

But I had another woman at home. I finally made it back to Miami, where I showed Regina some of the "bonus" money I'd made and told her, "See? I told you everything in Atlanta was going good. And there'll be a lot more of this, baby."

Regina was thrilled. We made love that night, and she was like a sexual dynamo. I guess I was, too, with all that pent-up energy from the traffic stop, the mental rush from the bank job, and the tantalizing visions of Tiana all still surging through my body. Afterward I lay in the dark wondering how Regina would react if she knew her husband was a bank robber. By morning she was already talking about a new house. She wanted a custom-built one. Told me it had always been her dream. And so my life was business as usual. Regina wanted a new house, I still wanted to live the high life, and the strip club girls required money, money, money.

William and Ella Mae Purnell, my maternal grandparents

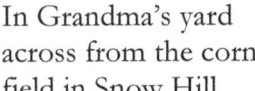

In Grandma's yard across from the corn field in Snow Hill

Elementary school

Wilmington, Lancaster Avenue, West Side neighborhood

High school track race (*Wilmington Morning News*)

Barnhill joins Florida's Delaware track pipeline

Heading to Florida (*Wilmington Morning News*)

Gator!

USA Track & Field Championship, 1983

That's me coming on strong from the outside

Shaking President Criser's hand at University of Florida graduation

With family at graduation

Working as Administrative Assistant in UF Athletic Department

With two-year-old Larry Jr., on the rocks at Miami Beach

At work as event coordinator at Miami Arena

Leisure Management executive profile

Assistant Executive Director,
Orange Bowl Committee staff, all-access badge

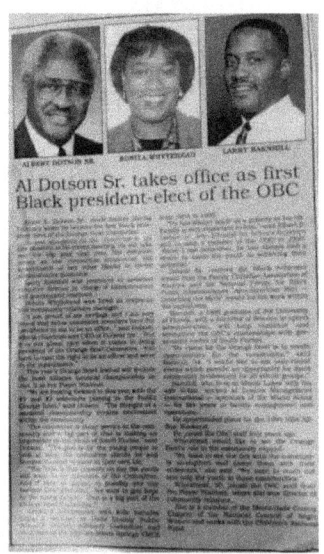

Announcement of my promotion to Assistant Executive Director
Administration & Government Relations
(courtesy of the *Miami Times*)

"The Unusual Suspects," *The Atlanta Journal-Constitution*

Car crash site after chase (source: FBI)

Money cannisters and water tub for dye packs (source: FBI)

Money cannisters (source: FBI)

One of the money bags (source: FBI)

At FCI-Coleman, A-League basketball championship

At FCI-Coleman, family visitation

Visitation with co-author Jerry Payne and cousin Leonard "Swan" Mason. FCI Jesup, Georgia

14

POTENTIAL

For the Orange Bowl, 1996 was a big year. The Summer Olympics were held in Atlanta that year, but some of the qualifying events were held in other venues in other cities. We hosted some of the qualifying soccer matches, and this meant trips to Atlanta for meetings with the International Olympic Committee and the Atlanta Committee for the Olympic Games. Once again, I was rubbing shoulders with VIPs, meeting men like Billy Payne, president and CEO of the Atlanta Committee for the Olympic Games. Later Payne would go on to chair the illustrious Augusta National Golf Club.

It also meant access to the events in Atlanta. I had a notebook full of complimentary tickets, and I took my son to watch some of the track and field, basketball, and volleyball events. It was a magical couple of weeks, marred unfortunately by the setting off of a pipe bomb in Olympic Park. The bomb killed one person and injured one hundred eleven.

A domestic terrorist was eventually charged after setting off more bombs in 1997 and 1998, but Richard Jewell, the security guard who first spotted the bomb, was the one the FBI initially went after, more or less ruining the guy's life.

I was in the park that night, listening to the musical acts playing there, but I was three stages away from the stage where the bomb went off. I never heard the explosion over the music, but I saw the people running from that direction, and soon cops were herding us out of the park. It wasn't until later that I learned what had happened.

But there was more going on for me in Atlanta than the Olympics. I was enjoying the games and meeting with important people during the day, but by night I was busy doing something else: reconnaissance. I was meeting with Brads and Cannon and Taylor. We were making plans. We had banks to rob, and the Olympics was the perfect cover for me, a legitimate reason for me to be in Atlanta. We took trips to nearby towns like Conyers and Roswell, scouting out the locations for our next scores, tentatively scheduled for early '97.

The guys would drop me back off at the hotel each night, and the next morning I'd slip back into my white-collar life, a solid citizen and proud representative of the Orange Bowl Committee. Nobody could have had any idea who I really was. In fact, at one point, while talking to some local Atlanta people on the committee, the subject of the Morning Glory

Boys came up. The '95 robberies were still fresh on everyone's minds. Nobody could believe that the robbers hadn't been caught. I nodded along. "Yeah, that's crazy stuff," I said, and then I tried to change the subject.

By then the Morning Glory Boys were on everybody's radar. The media had done stories on the heists. The banking industry's newsletter, *Bankers' Hotline*, had published articles, advising their members how to guard themselves against "morning glory" robberies. The FBI was warning banks too, and Special Agent Jeff Holmes was busy getting nowhere. We would find out later, to our amusement, that the professionalism and sophistication of our methods suggested to the FBI that we were most likely sponsored by a terrorist state, the robberies helping to fund their terrorist agenda. The World Trade Center bombing had taken place in 1993, and American intelligence agencies were on high alert. Of course the perception that we were somehow involved in international terrorism wasn't hurt by the fact that they had traced Cannon's gun to a Middle Eastern shop owner. But there was also a theory that we might be part of a domestic terror group. Witnesses reported we were Black. Maybe we were funding some radical Black militant organization. Or maybe we were Black Muslims. The only theory that didn't seem to be on the table was that the Morning Glory Boys were successful

American businessmen interested in robbing banks for no other reason than putting lots of green in their pockets.

We kept to our plans, and in 1997 we started off the year by hitting three more banks around the Atlanta area. Two we pulled off flawlessly. The third wasn't so smooth. We entered the bank like normal and took control in our usual way. Taylor called the manager by name and asked for the vault key. So far, so good. But when the manager retrieved the key, she must have pushed the silent alarm. We all saw the phones light up.

"Here," she said to Taylor, dangling the key in front of him with a sly grin on her face. Taylor glanced at the phone on her desk, its lights flashing. Then he looked back at the manager. Clearly, she knew that Taylor understood what the lights meant. That explained the sly grin as she continued holding out the key, tempting him to take it, to spend precious time in the vault with the cops on their way.

Taylor smiled back at her, then couldn't help but chuckle. "Okay, boys," he said, still maintaining eye contact with the manager. "I guess we'd better forget this one."

We hustled out the door, jumped into the car, and took off, laughing about the encounter. "Sometimes you just have to tip your cap," I said.

The two banks were enough, however. We'd each raked in enough cash to keep us satisfied for the conceivable future.

Turns out, that wasn't as long as I thought. Back in my civilian life, things weren't running so smooth. There was another director on the Orange Bowl Committee who had become a rival. Simon was politically connected in nearby Broward County and had brought a lot of sponsors in from the area. I didn't like Simon. I didn't trust him. I might have been ambitious, but Simon was power hungry and self-serving, the kind of guy who'd stop at nothing to get what he wanted. His main goal seemed to be driving a wedge between Kevin and me. Kevin didn't see it. He saw the money Simon was bringing in, but he couldn't see the risk. Simon had no loyalty. Simon was all about Simon. I could see that if things ever went south, Kevin would be the one taking the hit and Simon would go ahead and let him. I was the only one who had my old friend's back.

What it all led to was an almost impossible hostility between Simon and me. We couldn't work together. Kevin tried to smooth things over one night, asking us both to dinner at Shula's Steakhouse. But in the course of that dinner, I heard Kevin talk glowingly about Simon. It was as though I was solely to blame for the animosity. Across the table I watched Simon smile smugly at me. He knew he'd ingratiated himself with Kevin at my expense, and he was loving every second of it. So much for loyalty. Kevin had made his choice. Turns out that money can create bad choices, even if they aren't illegal.

Now, none of this would have meant shit if I had just committed entirely to a career as a bank robber. Who needed it? But even then—even after robbing all the banks I'd robbed—I still, unbelievably, didn't see myself as a bank robber. Or any kind of criminal. My self-image was that of a businessman. And I was going to succeed *in business*.

For that to happen, I knew, given the Orange Bowl situation, that I needed to start my own company and be my own boss. It wasn't as if I hadn't thought about it. I'd been feeling an entrepreneurial tug for a while. I'd been stuck at the same salary, and I knew that if I had my own company working out contracts for the Orange Bowl, I'd be making commissions that could exceed what I was being paid by five or ten times. And I had the contacts.

I became a registered lobbyist in Miami and Dade County, and I broke the news to Regina that I was leaving the Orange Bowl to pursue promotion and merchandising opportunities on my own. Initially she didn't understand why a person would leave a sure thing, but she supported me when she started seeing the possibilities.

I kept my relationship with Kevin intact. He had status, contacts, and business know-how. In fact, he became an equity partner in my new venture. I also partnered with a local business merchandiser by the name of Derek Hughes. Derek was special events concessionaire for the Orange Bowl, and we'd worked together for years. He and I began working on a multimillion-dollar licensing deal with the Dade County School Board. I had an in. Regina's father was a regional superintendent with over twenty-five years of service. I was able to get behind doors with the people who made the major financial decisions for Dade County Public Schools, including the superintendent. We showed them the financial benefits of using logos and trademarks. "Dade County Public Schools can be a pioneer in alternative funding generation for high school programs," we told them in a presentation. "Our company will oversee the production of quality merchandise, thereby generating significant revenue for the school system."

After months of lobbying and meetings, we won the approval of the school board. It was a huge deal, and the night of the award, I took Regina and her parents out to dinner at an exclusive restaurant in the Bal Harbour Shops in North Miami to celebrate.

The possibilities didn't stop there. Soon after that my company was shortlisted as one of two groups invited to make presentations to the city of Homestead, Florida, to manage and market their multipurpose arena. The presentation went well, and over the course of the next few weeks, we continued discussions with the city manager.

But all this time I was still living the high life. Clubs, girls, coke. The difference was, I no longer had a steady source of income. What I had was *potential*. But you can't spend potential, and before long the bank money dwindled down to nothing.

Then everything got worse. During this time Regina and I were trying to start a family. Of course I had my son, but Regina wanted a baby that would be ours. But we had trouble conceiving. Ultimately, Regina was diagnosed with endometriosis, a uterine disorder that was more or less rendering her infertile. Her doctor recommended in vitro fertilization, an expensive procedure, but we were both committed to having a child, and I was sure that the money from my new business would be coming in anytime. *Potential.*

The money quickly became even more of a non-issue when, during the implantation procedure, Regina began hemorrhaging. You don't think of money when it's life and death. I was there, dressed in a surgical gown and cap, holding Regina's hand for support, when suddenly the procedure somehow went very wrong. "What's happening?!" Regina cried out as the hemorrhaging began. The next thing I knew, I was being ushered out the door while an anesthesiologist was being ushered in. The scene became chaotic, with nurses and doctors springing into action for what turned out to be emergency surgery. Somebody shoved a clipboard in my face telling me I needed to sign the form so that they'd have permission to "save Regina's life." It might have been the most frightened I'd ever been.

An hour later Regina was resting comfortably, with the doctor assuring us we could still try to conceive.

"It's gonna be okay," I whispered to Regina after the doctor left the room.

"We can try again?"

"That's what the man said."

Regina began to cry.

"Shhh," I said, putting my arm around her. "It's gonna happen."

"But we can't afford it."

"That's on me, babe. That ain't nothin' you gotta think about. Just trust me, okay? Now let's get dressed and get the hell out of here."

By then Regina's father had made it to the hospital. He took her out to the car while I stopped at the receptionist's desk to settle the bill.

"That's $15,552," she said, almost apologetically.

I smiled and handed her my American Express card, feeling a knot in my stomach and a tightness in my chest that I tried hard not to show. I kept the cool expression even after she told me the card had been rejected. "Hmm . . . that's odd. Well, here," I said, handing her a Visa card. "Can you split it over two cards?" That seemed to work, but I left not knowing how in the hell I was going to pay the credit card bills when they came due. But Regina was okay. That was the main thing.

In the days and weeks to come, however, money would become the major driving force of my life. That's the way it is when you run out of it. The promise of business from the Dade County School System and the city of Homestead was all tied up in politics and red tape. Progress had ground to a crawl.

My lifestyle, even without the clubs and girls and coke, didn't help. Regina and I were still living in the upscale housing development that we'd moved into after our wedding, a neighborhood of wealthy businesspeople and professional athletes. We had nice cars. By then I was driving a Jaguar. We dressed well. I had dozens of suits and dress shoes. I justified it all by telling myself I needed it for my career. Mine was a perception business. I had to convey an image of success. In truth, though, I liked the way I looked in monogrammed shirts and cufflinks, and I liked driving down the streets of Miami in a pricey car.

I tried to keep our financial situation from Regina, but she wasn't blind. She didn't know about the strip club visits, which I'd covered by telling her I needed to entertain various clients, but she noticed the checking account getting low. I was late a few times with the house payment. I kept telling her it was going to be all right, but one night she put it all on the table: "Look, Larry," she said, "I just need to know. Can you take care of me or not?"

15

DOING THE LAUNDRY

"Don't worry about a thing, baby," I told Regina with a smile. "Of course I can take care of you."

But the smile was forced. What Regina didn't know was that I was also taking care of another life, a life that included partying hard at all the finest places around. As if my life with Regina wasn't expensive enough. She still wanted a custom-built house. She wanted a baby, and the in vitro treatments were going to cost a fortune, with no guarantees. She also started talking about opening her own business—a learning academy/nursery. It was a great idea. Except that she'd need investment capital. Where was that going to come from?

In the meantime, I was still trying to get my own business off the ground. But things were slow. Regina didn't understand slow. Truthfully, neither did I. The money from the bank heists was a two-edged sword. It provided a comfortable lifestyle where money was no object, but then it spoiled a person for any hope of being able to handle delayed gratification. Regina wanted it all now, and I started finding myself feeling the same way. The difference was that Regina had no idea how our lifestyle was being financed. She thought the business was running well. I showed her the money, and she started planning on what we were going to do with it. I had set up unrealistic expectations for the both of us.

And of course it wasn't just Regina. I'd fooled everyone. My family back in Wilmington all knew me as a highly successful business executive. I had VIP seating from NBC every year for the Macy's Thanksgiving Day Parade, and I'd bring family members with me. I'd fly them down for the Orange Bowl and the Orange Bowl Parade too. In their eyes—in everybody's eyes—I was a winner.

But I knew what was fueling it all, and the stress of living the lie was overwhelming. I found relief in those wild nights out at the clubs throwing money at strippers. Which, of course, only added to the stress when the bills came due.

Maybe that's why I eventually found solace in the arms of Tiana.

Tiana hadn't left my mind since I'd met her at the Hilton in Fort Lauderdale. We'd kept in touch—a phone call here, a lunch there. At first there was nothing physical between us. We were becoming good friends. She talked to me a lot about her personal life. Tiana had it hard. I'd been to her house, the duplex she and her son shared with a couple of friends. It was cramped and in a dicey neighborhood. She wanted to get out of the strip clubs, but she needed the money. Besides her son, she was taking care of her sister, who was HIV positive, and trying as best she could to help pay for her medications. I gave Tiana money from time to time.

It wasn't long before I started feeling something more than friendship for Tiana. Turns out, she had similar feelings for me. One night we made love. It was slow and tender. This wasn't the sex I was used to having with girls, not even with Regina. This was special. We made love all night, and by the morning, I knew I had another woman in my life.

The heart was happy.

The wallet groaned like an old man.

The long and the short of it was that there was no way I could fund my lifestyle without robbing banks. What had started out as a one-time deal to catch up on my finances had become a career that I now depended upon. There was no getting out of it.

And so, the Morning Glory Boys remained in action. There were more heists. More getaways. More duffels of cash. Each time seemed less risky than the last. We knew the FBI wasn't getting anywhere close to discovering who we were. And the manner in which we pulled off each job was so fluid that we could have done it in our sleep.

The only part that seemed risky to me was the actual spending of the cash. Buying big-ticket items with stacks of hundreds and fifties tends to raise flags. Of course it helped that my business was, in large part, a cash business. There were no flags raised when I'd take cash to the bank to put into my business account, as long as I wasn't depositing a bunch all at once. In fact, banks are required to report to the federal government any deposit over $10,000. So, I'd deposit $5,000 one week, maybe $6,000 the next. Enough over time to write checks against for whatever I needed.

More incriminating was the cash itself. A lot of the money we took in was new—straight off the press with sequential serial numbers. Easy to trace, in other words.

I volunteered to be a broker for the gang. My business traveling afforded me an excuse to fly to Las Vegas from time to time. After all, conventions were always being held there—great opportunities to network for my company. And sometimes I'd do just that. But mostly what I did was take care of the money. For a small percentage, Cannon, Taylor, and Bradley would give me their shares of the latest bank take. I'd go to the casinos, use the money to buy chips, gamble a little, and then exchange the chips for cash—random cash, not the sequential bills from the banks. The casinos now had those. One time I even took Regina and bankrolled us a four-day vacation.

I never tried to clean all the cash in one visit, so my trips to the casinos were frequent. People began to recognize me, and the dealers and other members of the staff knew my name. One day, at the main casino I went to, the pit manager, a well-dressed, Italian-looking gentleman, approached me and said, "Hello, Mr. Barnhill."

"Hi," I said. I'd never met the pit boss before, but apparently my visits had registered with him.

"You know," he said, lowering his voice, "I can help you with your situation."

I felt my stomach knotting. "My situation?"

"We can take care of it in a more, well, let's say 'professional' manner?"

I put on my best perplexed expression and said, "I'm sorry, I really don't know what you mean."

"Mr. Barnhill," he continued. "You come in here over the course of three or four days, several times a day. You bring a lot of cash; you gamble only a little."

"Yes, well, you see, I'm in the promotional business, catering to the entertainment industry. It's a business that deals in cash quite a bit. Here's my card. And I'm afraid I'm not much of a gambler. I like to try my luck in between client appointments. It helps me pass the time."

The pit boss wasn't buying. But how did I know he was just a pit boss? For all I knew, the man could have been undercover FBI.

"Just the same," he said, "here's *my* card. If you ever want to sit down and discuss business, I do hope you'll get in touch with me."

I took the card, maintaining my calm but dropping the confused expression. This guy knew what I was doing, and I knew that any denials at this point would seem silly. "Thanks," I said. "I'll remember that."

Back in Florida, Tiana told me one night that she was quitting the club. She didn't want to dance anymore. She said she was done stripping for men and she wanted something better for herself. Only problem was, until Tiana could find something, she had no source of income. She didn't know how she was going to make the rent on the cramped duplex. "Leave it to me," I told her. Before the next month's rent was due, I found Tiana a three-bedroom house, signing the lease myself. There was enough room for her and her son and her sister. She was ecstatic.

For me it was just one more financial obligation. The bank money would take care of it. At least until the business took off, which, I kept telling myself, would be any day.

One afternoon I got a phone call. "Mr. Barnhill?"

"Yes?"

"You might remember me. We met in Las Vegas." It was the pit boss from the casino. He'd kept my card. Turned out his name was Carl and he was coming to Miami on vacation with his family. Did I have any advice for a good resort hotel, preferably with a golf course? I had a sense Carl wanted more than that. I went into professional businessman mode and told him I could do a lot better than advice. The Orange Bowl was coming up and I still had contacts there. I could get him seats to the game if he wanted, as well as passes to the other festivities. Then I hooked him up with a contact at the Doral Golf Resort. I assured Carl he'd be well taken care of.

"Thanks," he said. "Why don't I give you a call when I'm in town. We can meet for a drink."

There it was. Carl wanted to pursue the proposition he'd offered at the casino. I was intrigued, but I still wasn't sold. I knew the FBI was out there. How much did they know about the Morning Glory Boys? They could never catch us in the act and had virtually zero leads on who we were. It stood to reason that their best opportunity to track us down was to either look for someone's irregular spending habits or to investigate someone trying to launder money by, say, cashing it in for chips at a Las Vegas casino and then cashing back out. It wasn't hard to imagine that the casino in question might have tipped off the Feds. In turn, they'd plant a man at the casino, disguised as a pit manager with a little side business.

It might have seemed a bit paranoid on my part, but a little paranoia can be a good thing. I figured a little paranoia might just keep me out of prison.

Either way, I knew I needed to meet with Carl. If he was sincere, I could sure use the help. After all, if he had spotted what I was doing at the casino, so could others. And if he was FBI and I acted spooked, that would be a red flag and the Feds would probably start following me everywhere I went.

"Sure," I said. "Maybe we can even get a round of golf in."

"I'd like that."

We made plans. Two weeks later, on a sunny Friday morning, I met Carl at the pro shop at Doral. Before the two of us hit the links, he introduced me to his wife and two kids, who had just finished breakfast. Then we jumped into our golf cart.

I hadn't expected to meet the family. What was the purpose of that? Was it calculated to make me feel more comfortable with Carl? To trust him more? To forge some kind of bond? If so, it was a good business move. But all those objectives would work just as well if Carl was an FBI agent trying to get me to open up. Sure, adding the family made for a pretty elaborate ruse, but that's exactly the sort of thing the FBI would do.

We had eighteen holes ahead of us. I planned to play things as cool as I could, but something told me I needed to trust

Carl. I hoped my intuition was right because it seemed to me that by the eighteenth hole, I'd either have a new business partner or be in handcuffs, headed downtown.

16

WHAT HAPPENS IN VEGAS

For the first nine holes, we made small talk. We chatted about politics and sports. Carl told me about his background and his family. We exchanged stories and laughed about our equally wild college days, and he told me how he'd ended up in Vegas. By the tenth hole, we'd both had a couple of beers and were starting to loosen up.

Carl finished a putt and said, "Do you mind if I smoke?"

"Not at all." I was thinking of lighting a cigar myself. But as we got in the cart, I saw that Carl's cigarette was no ordinary cigarette. Carl had pulled a joint out of his pocket.

"You still don't mind?" he grinned.

I laughed. "Hey, do your thing, man. As long as you don't mind me doing my thing." As Carl drove, I slipped my personal bag of cocaine out of my pocket. When Carl asked for a hit, I thought, *If this guy is undercover FBI, he sure is taking the part seriously.*

We finished up our game and then had a couple more beers in the clubhouse. Then Carl said he needed some time to chill before hooking back up with the family, and it occurred to me that this was a man living two lives just like me. His wife didn't know he smoked weed or did coke, and she sure as shit didn't know he helped criminals launder money.

"But, Larry," he said, "maybe we can get together later tonight. I'm going to have dinner with the wife and kids, but, man, I'd love to spend some time hanging out in South Beach. I got a feeling you know all the right places."

"Sure, man. You can't beat the Miami night life. I'll call you later when I'm on my way."

"That sounds great, but we better call a limo, don't you think?"

A limo? Carl was my kind of guy. "I'll take care of it," I said.

I had dinner with Regina, then told her I had to entertain my new "client" for the night. Regina understood. She always understood, as long as the money kept coming in. But she didn't let me out of the house without us having sex first. It was her way of reminding me who I belonged to.

That night Carl and I cruised up and down Collins Avenue and Ocean Drive, bar hopping all along the way, drawing the looks of the people on the street as we'd slide out of our limo, two well-dressed, obviously well-heeled gentlemen out on the town.

At one point Carl smiled and said, "So what other kind of clubs do you have in this town?"

"I know just the spot," I said, and told the driver to head for Club Rolexx.

In the VIP area Carl made himself at home, and I could tell he wasn't new to this kind of place, or this side of life, for that matter. And I was beginning to see that that was the point. Carl was equally at home in a tuxedo rubbing shoulders with the high-society types who might frequent his casino as with Black street gangsters and strippers. And he wanted me to know that.

Finally, in the limo back to Doral, he brought up the subject I'd been expecting all night. "You know it's not safe, Larry. You can't keep buying large amounts of chips and then turning them in for different cash. Both the FBI and DEA look for that kind of action. They know what it means. If you're not careful, it'll be just a matter of time before they pay you a visit and start asking a lot of uncomfortable questions."

I looked Carl in the eye and said, "Is this one of those visits?"

Carl laughed hard, then turned serious. "Larry, if I was FBI and this was one of those visits, we would have ended it a long time ago."

"Okay," I said. "I'm listening."

"We'll take a fifteen percent fee for cleaning your money. You don't need to know how. Just like we don't need to know where the money comes from. All I'm concerned about is the amount of heat you might bring down on us. But if you're a professional at what you do, and I sense that you are, then I'm willing to work with you."

"Thanks, Carl. I'll have to talk it over with my associates."

"Sure. You know how to get a hold of me. Thanks for a great night."

The limo dropped Carl off and I asked to be taken to Tiana's. Maybe I belonged to Regina, but at three o'clock in the morning, who's to say who really belongs to who?

Two days later I flew to Atlanta to meet with Cannon, Taylor, and Brads. I laid out the proposition, telling them twenty percent, giving me something extra for my trouble. These guys had been robbing banks before I'd joined the gang, so I knew they had stacks of cash hidden away that could use a good rinse. It took a while to convince them, but in the end they agreed, knowing that spending the money could be just as risky as giving it to someone to clean.

"I trust this guy," I assured them. "He's the real deal."

That night Taylor and I went out and hit the town, and he mentioned something about pulling off the next jobs right after New Year's, 2000. It was the millennium year, he said, and then he started talking about the Y2K thing, telling me the banks would be flush with cash right at the start of the year. I wasn't really listening. I had enough going on without having to think about our next heist. Besides, I wasn't totally committed to another bank job. Once my business got on its feet, I would leave that world behind. I was a legitimate businessman, after all. I didn't need to rob no fucking banks. Well, I mean, not forever.

I left Atlanta with $100,000 from each of the guys, then made another trip to Vegas with $100,000 of my own. Carl came to my hotel room at the Mirage, picked up the 400 grand, and handed me a duffle bag that contained $340,000 in cash, keeping the agreed-upon difference as his commission. Then we agreed to get together later that night to paint the town.

Just the same, I left the Mirage shortly after Carl left and checked into another hotel off the strip. Maybe it was that paranoia again, but I didn't want anyone to know where I was staying, even Carl.

A few hours later we met for dinner and drinks. Afterward Carl said, "Where's Elvis?" Elvis was his nickname for coke.

"Elvis is right here," I said, pulling out my bag.

We did some coke and then did some bar hopping, winding up, predictably, at a strip club, throwing more money around. Carl, after all, had just made a cool $60,000. He dropped me off at the Mirage in the wee hours of the morning, and I grabbed a cab back to my hotel.

The next day, I flew to Atlanta and doled out the clean cash to the Morning Glory Boys. There would be more trips to Vegas as we exchanged our money—one hundred grand each at a time.

Back in Miami I was trying to run a business and, essentially, maintain two households. The pressure was getting to me. I started dropping weight. I was tired all the time. The coke picked me up when I needed it but slammed me back down afterward. The partying kept my mind occupied and served as an escape, but when the morning came around, the stress would come back tenfold.

Of all the things I needed to give up, I knew that bank robbing had to be the first. But not just yet. On one of those trips back to Atlanta from Vegas, this one toward the end of 1999, I heard more about the Y2K bank idea. Rumor had it that the Fed was printing an extra $50 billion. Banks would be up to their ceilings with cash, just in case computers around the world crashed, as some people thought. The plan was to hit five banks the first week of January. We figured each would be worth a cool million at the least.

I went along with the plan, knowing it would be the last of the robberies for me. We all felt the same way. One week, five banks. And then the Morning Glory Boys would ride off into the sunset. I'd get my business going, get my personal life squared away, give up the coke and the strippers and the partying, and live a respectable life. Yes sir, the sun was coming up on the new millennium, and I was ready for it. The year 2000 was going to be my year.

17

BUSTED

The FBI was stumped, but not completely clueless. Later we would learn that they had noticed an uptick in carjackings shortly before the bank robberies. I never asked where Cannon and Taylor got our getaway cars, but I would eventually discover that they targeted drivers who pulled up to outside mailboxes at apartment complexes. The FBI noticed the pattern. The carjackings were always followed by the bank heists.

They noticed another pattern. The banks were typically First Union banks. We kept hitting those because they were all similarly laid out. When January 2000 came around, based on recent carjacking reports, the FBI was able to credibly predict the robbery of a First Union bank. Later they claimed they even knew that the First Union bank of Lilburn was one of the more likely targets. Did they really know this? Who can say? The FBI files are unavailable today, but it would explain the quick appearance of the cop that day. The citizen who was in the drive-through lane that morning was named Terry

Chastain. Chastain looked in and saw a masked man behind the counter—Taylor going for the Federal Reserve money. He could have called 911, but he didn't have to. He noticed a cop car that just happened to be sitting at a diner adjacent to the bank. Coincidence? Maybe not. Either way, Chastain left the drive-through and drove straight toward the cop car, occupied by Lilburn police officer Ben Chitwood.

Taylor had gone back behind the counter after asking the manager specifically about the Y2K money. "It's in the receiving safe," she'd replied, "but the key is in the vault." From my post at the door, I looked at the watch and saw that we were coming close to time. But the Y2K money—that was my ticket out. I'd be on Easy Street from then on. I'd go back to Florida, infuse the business with some much-needed cash, and live the life of an honest, successful businessman. *Get the fucking money*, I thought. *Let's go.*

I couldn't see Chastain from my position, and I'm guessing Taylor didn't either. When he pulled in beside Officer Chitwood and told him what he saw, Chitwood radioed in that the First Union of Lilburn was being robbed. Every cop in the area was soon on their way, and it was no surprise. There wasn't a cop in the state who hadn't been made aware of the Morning Glory Boys. Plans were in place. For the cops, it was *go* time.

The diner parking lot was on a slight elevation from the bank, with a grassy rise between the two. After making the call, Chitwood eased his car to the edge of the rise, got out, and started walking down toward the entrance of the bank. That's when I first saw him. And he saw me. Our eyes met and I felt a chill run through my body. This was it. We needed to move.

"Five-O!" I called out.

Chitwood walked around the bank, looking in through the floor-to-ceiling windows to confirm Chastain's report. When he disappeared behind a brick wall separating two of the windows, we made a break for it out the front door, with Cannon and me the first ones out. Cannon actually had some of the bank's money—a duffle cross-slung over his shoulder with four cannisters of cash inside of it. We dove into the back seat of the getaway car. Taylor and Bradley were coming out of the bank just as Chitwood reappeared around the corner. They'd taken off their masks, and that's when they waved toward the bank behind them, suggesting to Chitwood that the robbers were still inside, the kind of lame-ass move you make when you've got nothing else. Chitwood knew better.

Taylor peeled our getaway car out of the parking lot, and Chitwood called into his radio, letting everyone know we were mobile. Then he went inside to check on the employees and customers. At least that's what the police report would later state. I could have sworn he ran back up that grassy hill to get in his car and give chase. Truthfully, things started happening so fast, no one could have possibly kept track. But nobody disagrees that right at that moment Officer Carmen Ivan came upon the scene. She'd heard Chitwood's report and came barreling into the bank parking lot, tires squealing. So did Lilburn police sergeant Rob Worley. Worley blocked one exit with his vehicle and sprang out of the car with his gun drawn. Ivan placed her car at the other exit but left a space, wisely deciding against blocking us in completely, knowing a dangerous shootout could be the only result. In an interview with the *Atlanta Journal-Constitution* a few days later, she'd quote her grandfather, who always told her, "Never corner a rat, because they will go for the throat."

But that didn't stop her from pulling out her gun and taking a standing position behind her open driver's-side door. Taylor drove right at her, and he and Bradley drew their guns. Bradley came out with a long gun. And that's when shots were fired, back and forth. *This is it*, I thought. *We're in it now. For fucking keeps.* It wasn't just bank robbing anymore. It was life and death for everyone involved. We were going to get away or we were going to die trying. And maybe even kill.

Taylor swerved around Ivan's car but caught the door, which slammed into her, dislocating her finger and giving her a couple of nasty bruises on the elbow and leg. Nevertheless, she was able to spin around and get a shot off as our car sped out of the parking lot, hitting our car and shattering the back windshield. "God*damn!*" someone said.

"Go!" Cannon screamed. "Fucking *go!*"

Taylor sped out of the lot while Ivan jumped into her car and followed, only noticing then, according to her report, that her finger was bent in an L shape. Also following, as I would later learn, was Officer Tony Menichini, who'd heard the call too. He'd come to the scene just as we were pulling out. Chitwood had given a description of the car and Menichini gave chase. Menichini called out our location and direction, and that's when seemingly every police officer in Georgia converged on us.

Taylor accelerated onto Lawrenceville Highway. Menichini kept up.

"Taylor, man, you gotta fucking lose this guy," said Bradley.

"What the fuck you think I'm tryin' to do?!"

Taylor veered from lane to lane, weaving in and out of traffic. Cannon and I were being tossed around in the back seat. I turned, and through the blown-out rear window, I could see the flashing lights of the cars chasing us. Then Taylor nudged a van, causing it to spin around and slow the traffic behind us. From the far-left lane, he swerved right, taking the car across two lanes and turning us onto Rockbridge Road. The maneuver created even more havoc behind us, and when I looked back through the window, it didn't appear as if anybody was following anymore. I breathed a sigh of relief. Cruising along Rockbridge, with its tall trees lining the road, it occurred to me that maybe we were going to make it after all. *Just get me through this*, I thought. *And that will be it. No more fucking banks. Ever.*

Then came the blowout, what I at first thought was a gunshot.

"Fuck!" said Taylor, wrestling with the steering wheel.

Up ahead I suddenly saw more lights. Behind us, even more. Now they were coming at us from both directions.

"Get us into the woods!" I yelled out. If we could just get lost in the woods, stay out of sight of the helicopter, which I knew had to be on its way. In fact, I would learn later that the Georgia Bureau of Investigation had its chopper pilots on standby, anticipating a robbery by the Morning Glory Gang. Once they saw us, I knew it would be all over. There would be TV news choppers too. Nobody wanted to miss this story. But if we could get through the woods and come out the other side, maybe we could beat the odds. There was a reason Taylor had chosen Rockbridge. We weren't far from where I'd parked my truck.

"Get ready," Cannon said. "If they get to us at the woods, we gonna have to shoot it out."

"Gotta do what we gotta do," said Bradley.

Taylor brought us to a stop at the edge of the woods and we burst out of the car. By then Menichini was upon us, having somehow gotten around the traffic mess we'd caused. He jumped out of his car and pulled his service revolver. "Stop!" he yelled. We ran for the woods, with Cannon turning and firing. Menichini shot back, but with more cops on their way, we couldn't stop and shoot it out like Cannon had said. We needed to keep moving, and that's when we split up, with Cannon and Taylor going one way and me and Bradley going the other.

Menichini, according to the report, stopped at that moment and waited for backup. He didn't have to wait long. Officer Carmen Ivan, battered and bruised, hadn't stopped chasing us. Neither had Worley. Chitwood was on his way, too, along with every other cop around. Plus, the FBI was now on the scene. For years they'd been waiting for this moment—the moment when the Morning Glory Gang would trip itself up.

The rest plays out in my mind like it was yesterday. Bradley and I are in the woods. We cut across the grove of trees and I can feel my heart pounding and my lungs aching for breath. None of the training we'd done matters now. There's nothing in the playbook for a chase on foot with cops coming from everywhere. I'm in survival mode. I'm in the moment, a zone, my senses heightened and my mind on autopilot. I have to make it to freedom; it's my only thought.

We get to the far end of the woods and stop at the edge of a small subdivision. Where to now? Then we spot a running car in the driveway of a house. It's our only chance. "Move!" says Brads, and we take off for the car. At that moment a police car, siren blaring, comes around the corner and starts speeding right at us. Seeing us, the driver slams on the brakes and comes to a stop. I try to stop, too, but my momentum carries me to the hood of his vehicle. I push off and spin around, following Bradley back into the woods.

Behind us Seargent Donny Kelly steps out of his car and raises his gun. "Stop!" he yells.

I keep going, waiting for a bullet in the back, certain it will come. Maybe it wounds me; maybe it kills me. Maybe it wakes me out of this insane fucking nightmare I'm having.

Kelly shoots but he misses. I'm still alive. And still in the nightmare. Once back in the woods, we run parallel to the road we'd come in on, but we know we can't stay in the woods forever. In fact, unknown to us, a cop with a K9 dog is en route. Bradley shoves his gun under some brush, but I still have mine in my fanny pack. Back on the other side of the woods, we spy a taxicab parked in the road. We move toward it, crouching behind some bushes at the edge of the tree line. I pull out my gun.

CONTROL. MOVE. DOMINATE.

What we don't know is that no more than twenty-five feet away, Officer Carmen Ivan is crouched down too. She sees us. She thinks about shooting but sees my gun drawn and doesn't know that Bradley has dropped his. She's certain we have more firepower and knows that a shot from her will trigger a gunfight that she might well lose. I'll have plenty of time later to think about that decision, and how it probably saved lives. Maybe hers. Maybe mine.

Meanwhile, Bradley turns to me. "The taxi," he says.

I nod.

The taxi driver notices the two men coming his way out of the trees, one waving a gun, and decides to defend himself by locking the doors and laying on the horn.

"Open up!" Bradley shouts.

I shoot at the ground. The police report will state that I shot at the taxi, but I have no intention of hurting the man.

"Open the fucking door!" Bradley shouts again, but the taxi driver throws the cab in reverse and speeds away from us just as more lights and sirens start coming down the street toward us, our position having been compromised by Ivan's latest radio report.

Now it's back to the woods, but once behind the trees, I decide I've had enough. There are cops on all sides of us now, closing in fast. I bury my gun under a pile of leaves and say to Brads, "Man, it's over."

He nods. "I know." But then he starts running some more.

Me, I do something reasonable for the first time in a very long while. I stop running and lay down on the ground and wait for it all to end.

18

COMMITTED

Thoughts of Regina went through my head. And Tiana. I thought about my business. My career. I thought about people like Kevin Goodman from the Orange Bowl. What was he going to think when he'd learn I was a criminal? I thought about my mother.

I thought about my son.

All these thoughts flashed before me as I waited for the inevitable. I didn't have to wait long. The K9 had arrived on the scene by then, and in no time a German Shepherd was on my pants leg.

"I don't have a gun!" I shouted out, hoping that would take away any excuse for some overzealous cop looking to be a hero to put a bullet in my head.

"Get up on your knees!" I heard from behind me. The K9 officer called the dog off me, and I raised myself to my knees with my arms up in the air. But then an officer rushed up behind me and shoved his foot in the back of my neck, forcing me headfirst back to the ground. I felt his gun against my head.

"Don't move," he said. Then he pulled my hands behind my back and slapped on the cuffs. He yanked me to my feet and pulled me along by my arm, out of the woods, and into the back seat of a waiting police vehicle. There, to my horror, I could hear the continued chase through the vehicle's radio. Cannon and Taylor were still on the run. Brads had been grabbed by then, but I didn't know it at the time. Out-of-breath officers would break in with urgent reports of where the suspects were: "He's behind a building!" I'd hear, or "One is running along the ravine!" Some of the calls were no doubt from the police chopper that had arrived on the scene by then. News choppers were hovering around as well. Through the static, I could hear the sounds of gunshots. Someone was going to get killed, I was sure of it. I whispered a quick prayer to a God I knew I hadn't paid much attention to. Maybe I had no right to ask, but I prayed for the gunshots to stop. I'd never wanted anyone to get hurt.

Out of the back seat window of the car I saw a black Suburban speeding toward us. Leaving a trail of rubber and dust, it screeched to a halt in front of our vehicle and a man got out of the driver's side and marched up to my door, threw it open, and leaned in close. Special Agent Jeff Holmes of the FBI was now on the scene.

"Who are you, and how many more are still out there?" he said, pulling his large gun out of its holster, making sure I could see it. I hesitated, but Special Agent Jeff Holmes was in no mood for hesitation. He leaned in even closer, his jaw clenched and his eyes narrowing. "Tell me what I want to know now, or I swear to Christ I will take your handcuffs off, send your Black ass back into the woods, and hunt you down like a wild animal."

I'd had enough time by then to concoct a story. It wasn't a very good one, but it was all I had. "There are five of us," I said. "But I'm only the driver." It was a Hail Mary. I knew witnesses would report four bank robbers. Maybe I could claim that I wasn't one of those four. That I'd never entered the bank. That I'd never held a gun.

"Take him," Holmes sneered to the arresting agent. Then he slammed the door shut and returned to his car, barking into the radio before taking off.

We drove to a staging area that the FBI had set up in the meantime, where I was transferred into a waiting FBI Suburban. That's when I saw Bradley being shoved into the back of another Suburban. I continued to listen to the chase on the radio like it was a Monday Night Football game. Finally, I heard a report that four men were in custody. They'd arrested Cannon and Taylor. I breathed a sigh of relief knowing no one had been hurt, but of course now there was chatter about the fifth person, the one I'd manufactured.

Cannon and Taylor were soon brought to the staging area, and there were black Suburbans for them too. Four men in custody, four Suburbans. They were already intent on keeping us apart; they didn't want to give us the chance to get our respective stories straight. But we'd planned for this, and we already had our story. We had no idea who the Morning Glory Boys were. This was our one and only robbery attempt. We were all drug and alcohol abusers and had decided in various states of intoxication that we needed to try to rob a bank. It was a one-time, off-the-cuff, spur-of-the-moment act, and we were all deeply sorry and ashamed. Sure, maybe some gunfire had been exchanged, but none of us shot our guns with the idea of actually hitting anybody. We'd just been trying to get away so we could resume our heretofore law-abiding lives. What we really needed was help for our addictions. Then we'd throw ourselves on the mercy of the court.

The success of the story hinged on one thing: we all had to stick to it.

While the search continued for the elusive fifth man, we were driven from the staging area to the Gwinnett County Correctional Institute to be processed. Then they separately interrogated each of us. Since I had said that I was the getaway driver, Holmes and two other agents put me back in one of the Suburbans and drove me around looking for my truck. I'd told them that's where we'd been heading, and their concern, presumably, was that the fifth man had made it to the truck and gotten away.

I wasn't much help. As we drove around, I pleaded ignorance of Atlanta's streets. "I'm from Florida. None of this looks familiar to me."

I'm not sure the matter of the truck was their first priority anyway. They had a suspect alone in the back seat of their vehicle, and the drive gave them an opportunity to press me some more. Holmes asked again about the fifth man's identity. "I just met him," I said. "I don't know his name. I don't really know any of these guys."

"What are you protecting them for?" Holmes asked. "We know all about you. Tell us what we want to know and things will go a lot easier for you."

"I told you everything." I knew there was no way they could have learned anything about me so quickly. Holmes was bluffing. Wasn't he?

After fruitlessly driving around, it was back to Gwinnett, where the interrogations continued. The theme was always the same: "Tell us everything you know and we can help you."

Holmes must have asked a dozen times if we were the Morning Glory Gang. A dozen times, I said, "I don't know what you're talking about."

"You're lying," he said at one point. "It turns out that we already know all about you guys anyway. One of your partners talked. Now it's time for you to tell us what *you* know."

I didn't say anything. Nobody talked, I was sure of it. We'd committed to that a long time ago.

By then the background checks had been completed. Holmes knew I was a businessman, a former official with the Orange Bowl Committee. An upstanding citizen.

"Tell me, Barnhill," he said, "what's a guy like you doing hiding in the woods after having tried to rob a bank? Come on, you're not like the other guys. Why are you helping them? Do you really think they give a shit about *you*?"

Another FBI agent started playing bad cop, screaming at me to come clean. "You shot at police officers and FBI agents!" he yelled, his face right up to mine. "You think you're ever going to see the outside of a prison cell?!"

"Are you the Morning Glory Gang?" Holmes repeated.

"I don't know what you're talking about."

"*Are you* the Morning Glory Gang?"

"Man, I don't even know what that is."

"Okay, Barnhill, so how do you know these guys?"

"I told you. Bradley is my cousin. I just came up to visit and he asked if I'd drive him and his friends to the bank. I met them this morning. I don't even know their names."

"Bullshit!" yelled the bad cop. "Tell us what you know!"

And so it went for several hours.

Finally, I was taken to a separate jail cell for the night. All of us were, each to his own cell, none of them in sight of each other. Mine was cold, the toilet didn't work, and the water barely ran in the sink.

I called for the officer in charge and told him about the toilet, and he said, "You're with the Morning Glory Gang, aren't you? You know, my brother is a cop, and he was out there today in the woods. You probably shot at him. And you're asking about the goddamn toilet? If I was out there today, I would have saved everyone the trouble. I'd have ended it all right there in the woods." Then he walked back to his station.

I climbed up on the bunk and lay there looking at the ceiling, thinking again about my life and all the people who were going to be shocked when they learned the truth about Larry Barnhill. I didn't sleep.

At five in the morning, I heard the clank of the cell door opening, and a guard came in. "Time to go," he said. "Time to face the judge for the arraignment and bond hearing." Then he snickered. "As if you're going to make bond."

The guard escorted me to a holding cell to wait for transportation. Once in the cell, I was given a bowl, a small bag of cereal, and a half-pint carton of milk. There, I saw the others being escorted into adjacent holding cells, still separated. After a long wait we were each led to a different vehicle. Each car had three FBI agents, two in the front seat, one in the back with the respective prisoner. Destination: the Richard B. Russell Federal Building and US Courthouse.

On the way the interrogations started up again. "Do you have any idea how serious things are for you right now?" the agent who was driving asked. Then he started talking about my accomplishments in life. "Listen, the other guys don't have as much to lose as you do. Why would you throw your life away for them?"

I stayed silent.

At the back entrance of the courthouse, it was a circus, with every media outlet in the county reporting on the saga of the Morning Glory Gang. Inside, it was off to another holding cell. Cannon and Bradley were in adjoining cells, and for the first time since the arrests, we were close enough to speak to each other, though we didn't need to say anything. We nodded at each other to indicate our personal commitments to staying the course, to stick to the story. Meanwhile, we weren't alone in these cells. Other alleged felons were awaiting their appearances before the judge, and every one of them seemed to know who we were, making us minor celebrities among the criminal population. Word of the shootout had gotten around.

Sometime during our wait, it struck me that Taylor wasn't there. It seemed strange, but then I figured that maybe there was another set of cells somewhere else. Taylor was no doubt waiting for his arraignment just like us, still committed, still loyal, still intent on sticking to the script.

19

ACDC

I pleaded not guilty at the arraignment and awaited the bond hearing. By then word had gotten out to friends and family, and a cousin in Atlanta, Leonard "Swan" Mason, soon found himself in the middle of it all. Swan had an auto repair and sales company. I'd hang out at his shop sometimes when I was in Atlanta. So would Bradley. Swan got to know Cannon and Taylor too. He'd come out to the strip clubs with us on occasion. But Swan knew nothing of the bank hits. I made sure of that, and so did Brads. We'd never wanted to get Swan involved.

Funny thing is, after everything hit the fan, Swan was able to look back and put the pieces together. Like how one night we were headed out to a club and I handed him a wad of money. A wad of *damp* money—bank bills that I'd plunged into the bucket of water that morning after one of the hits. Or the time he went out to get some auto parts and Brads rode along with him. On the way, Swan decided to swing by a bank. A *First Union* bank. A bank we'd robbed. He went through the drive-through lane and chatted with the girl at the window, noticing that Bradley kept his head turned away the whole time. Afterward Bradley, visibly angry, said, "Man, I didn't know you was goin' to the fuckin' bank!"

"What's the big deal?" Swan said.

Brads just shook his head and repeated, "Man, I didn't know you were goin' to the fuckin' *bank*."

He was even with us on the night we were at the Magic City nightclub and the undercover FBI agent was there asking about "T." He noticed we were all there one minute and gone the next, with nobody saying a thing. He'd also seen the way we threw money around when we went out. The strippers and the cocaine. A lot of nights, it was too much for him. He never asked, but by then he had assumed we were in the drug business. Later he would tell me that during those years, it was as if he barely recognized me as the cousin he'd known.

The unfortunate thing for Swan was that every one of us had his business card, something the FBI took note of. We'd done a great job of keeping our respective friends and families out of our business. They didn't even know each other. Swan, being cousin to both Bradley and me, was the exception, the common denominator of us four. He knew us all, and he'd hung with us all. He felt the heat almost immediately.

Swan and his wife had a place in New York, and that's where he'd been on the day of the arrest. It was Taylor's girlfriend who called and told him. In a state of disbelief, he flew back to Atlanta. By then media outlets had made their own connections. Swan drove to his shop but spun a 360 and drove away after seeing camera crews parked out front.

The FBI, meanwhile, was working on the theory that Swan was the fifth man. Not exactly as I'd described him—one of the four armed gangsters that held the banks up—but maybe as the money man. A lot of bank money was still unaccounted for, after all. And Swan's business would make a likely laundering operation; Swan often dealt in high-end cars. Plus, it seemed reasonable to the FBI that Swan could have helped supply the getaway vehicles.

There was a piece of potentially incriminating evidence too. Fortunately, the FBI never found it. Before going to New York, Swan had asked Brads to do him a favor and stick close to the shop. He was expecting payment from a customer on a car. A couple of times he called the shop to check on Brads, only to get the answering machine. He left messages: "Brads, don't forget the money, man. Get the money." What would the FBI have thought of *that*?

When Swan finally made it into his shop, the first order of business was to destroy the message tape. Good thing. Not long afterward two agents came to see him.

"You know why we're here?" one of them asked.

"Y'all want to buy a car?"

The agents weren't amused, and Swan got asked questions—lots of questions. They went through his bank records too. Swan would be a suspect for some time to come.

He wasn't the only one who felt some heat. Derek Hughes was the merchandiser I'd been working with for the multi-million-dollar licensing deal with the Dade County School Board. We'd become close friends. When the FBI went through my stuff, they found financial records that connected us. That's all they needed to call Derek in Miami. They told him they wanted to talk to him. Larry Barnhill had just been arrested for bank robbery after a shootout with law enforcement officers. A shocked Derek drove straight to the FBI building in North Miami Beach and told them they obviously had the wrong guy. They explained everything to him, then questioned him about the financial records. Maybe Derek's business was the money-laundering piece of the puzzle. Derek opened his books, giving them access to his checking account records and all his financials, and the FBI cleared him pretty quickly.

Kevin Goodman got a call from the FBI too. To give our merchandising company a little more credibility, I had listed him as president, and that gave the FBI another lead to follow. Kevin had been in New Orleans to attend the Sugar Bowl when his wife took a phone call from his executive assistant reporting my arrest. Kevin knew I hung out in the strip clubs and assumed that's where I'd gotten into some kind of trouble. When the assistant said it was for bank robbery, he was dumbfounded. Back at his hotel he went online. The internet wasn't fast or sophisticated back in 2000, but he still managed to find news articles of the arrest of a group known as the Morning Glory Gang. Trying to make sense of it, he called Regina, who was crying uncontrollably. Through sobs she said it was true and that the FBI was in our home at that very moment. Kevin went from dumbfounded to sick to his stomach.

It was only a few days later that the FBI called upon him in Miami, asking a lot of the same questions they'd asked Derek. And, like Derek, Kevin told them everything he knew, offering to open the books and give them whatever they needed. They pretty quickly realized Kevin didn't have anything to do with the merchandising company, but they became interested in any connections the Orange Bowl might have still had with me. In fact, the Orange Bowl Committee would eventually be subpoenaed.

Meanwhile, I was sitting tight in a cell at the Atlanta City Detention Center, informally known as ACDC. Friends and family were getting the news, and the prevailing belief was that surely some big mistake had been made. I'd been misidentified. Once the facts all came out, I'd be on my way home. Regina talked to her father, who was related to Willie Gary, a famous attorney known as the Giant Killer for taking down some of America's most well-known corporate giants. Gary in turn suggested a criminal defense lawyer and recommended Dwight Thomas, one of the best, with a track record of successfully defending high-profile clients.

Dwight came to ACDC and met with me, telling me not to say anything more to the FBI. "You shouldn't have even said there was a fifth man. You shouldn't have said anything at all. From now on, keep quiet and let me do the talking." And then he told me something else. There would be no bond. In fact, there was going to be a superseding indictment. The FBI had a witness who would corroborate the theory that we were the Morning Glory Gang. I wouldn't be on trial for one robbery—I'd be on trial for as many as two dozen over a ten-year period.

I suppose it shouldn't have come as a shock that the witness was Calvin Taylor. No wonder he wasn't in the holding cells for the arraignment. I'd find out later that he'd broken within hours of his arrest. When Holmes had said they already knew everything, he hadn't been bluffing. He'd just wanted my confirmation. As a point of procedure, he had to follow up on the idea that there may have been a fifth man, but he knew there wasn't one, unless you counted Swan.

I felt my heart sink. If I had even a shred of hope that our story might have helped mitigate an otherwise lengthy prison sentence, it dried up at that moment. My days of freedom were over. My life was over.

"What do we do?" I asked.

"Let's see how it plays out after the bond hearing," Dwight said. "Let's wait for the superseding indictment and see how the prosecutor approaches the case."

At the bond hearing, members of the media filled the hallway leading into the courtroom, and some of the reporters yelled out, "Are you the Morning Glory Gang?" I kept my head down. The main witness was Agent Jeff Holmes. Holmes testified that he had a signed affidavit from one of us stating that we were, in fact, the infamous Morning Glory Gang, and, further, we were responsible for twenty-three metro Atlanta robberies. Taylor sat there looking down at the floor. Judge Orinda Evans denied us bond (of course) and, pending the superseding indictment, we were led out of the courtroom and taken back to ACDC.

20

SENTENCING

Initially none of us were allowed visitors. Security was so tight that you'd have thought we were the Word Trade Center bombers of a few years before. I was out of my cell for only an hour a day for recreation, but I managed to at least make small talk with the rec supervisor. He was a former "Red Dog" agent, part of Atlanta's tough drug enforcement agency. Red Dog supposedly stood for Run Every Drug Dealer Out of Georgia. The supervisor would pass greetings back and forth between me and Brads. "Your cousin says, 'What's up?'" he'd tell me.

The superseding indictment required a grand jury hearing to determine what seemed inevitable to me: that there was probable cause to take our case to trial. Before then, they finally allowed family to visit. Everybody came one day, and in the visitor area behind a glass wall, I could talk by phone to them one at a time. They passed the phone around and all said the same things: "We'll get you out of this," "We know you're innocent," "That ain't you, Larry." My mom looked heartsick, but on the phone she was as upbeat as everybody else, and I tried to be just as positive back to her.

When it came time to talk to Regina, I told her the truth. I knew that the grand jury hearing meant friends and family and associates would all be subpoenaed and questioned. Everything was going to be laid bare. "Baby," I told Regina, "things are going to come out. I *was* involved."

"Larry, just listen to your attorney," she said. "We know it's going to be okay."

"Yeah, but there's more. They're going to talk about another woman." I knew Tiana would be subpoenaed. Our relationship, the house I was renting for her—it was all going to be brought up in court.

"Well, Larry, with all the traveling and late nights, I can't say it surprises me that you weren't being faithful."

How was it that I'd imagined I had been pulling something over on my wife all that time, that she hadn't at least been catching a glimpse of my other life?

The grand jury hearing came together pretty quickly, only about a month after our arrest. It seemed that anybody related to us in any way was subpoenaed to testify, all in a single, long, grueling day. Of course the FBI still couldn't believe that others weren't involved. In their minds there was no way the four of us could have kept everything so secret from everybody else. And so the strategy was to throw everybody together in a small waiting room. One by one, each person would be led out of the waiting room and into the courtroom. After testifying to the grand jury, each person would be brought back to the waiting room. That meant nobody went home. For twelve hours, some thirty people—related only in that they knew at least one of us—sat together in a cramped room. In-laws, wives, ex-wives, girlfriends. Pillars of society and strippers. We'd all lived double lives, and now those circles were colliding. You couldn't put a more motley group of people together if you tried. Anna, my first wife, was there. So was Regina. So was Tiana. Later I would hear of the tension in that room—the awkward silences, the scornful glares, the suspicious looks.

To the FBI, the surprising thing was that even with all that, they got nothing usable from all the testimonies. Nobody could shed any light on our crimes, and nobody else was evidently involved. For my part, I'd told everyone to just tell the truth. I had a chance to visit with Tiana beforehand. "Don't try to defend me," I said. "You'll just draw unnecessary suspicion to yourself." My advice was only partly for her benefit. Truthfully, I was still hanging on to the thread of hope that there would be no grounds to criminally pursue us as the infamous Morning Glory Gang and I didn't want any stories, no matter how well-intentioned, told to the grand jury that might be inconsistent with what I'd been saying about my "one-time involvement."

Regina didn't testify, invoking her privilege as a spouse to decline to answer any questions. Other relatives did, as did business associates, but the questioning of each was pretty short. The prosecutor, District Attorney Thomas Devlin, seemed satisfied with the testimonies of guys like Derek and Kevin. The businesses they represented were clearly not connected to the bank jobs. Still, it was embarrassing for Kevin to have to testify for the Orange Bowl Committee. Out in the hallway, media people were trying to take his picture. A couple of staff members who were with him ushered him into an elevator to get away from the reporters. I would find out later how much Kevin second-guessed himself for having so massively misjudged me. He knew I lived a fast life, that I liked the clubs and the women. He didn't know about the cocaine, though, and like everybody else, he could never have imagined the robberies.

Although Kevin's time on the stand was short, Swan was grilled a little harder. He was one of the last to go. They'd kept him waiting until close to six in the evening, turning him into a nervous wreck. Finally, they got him on the stand.

"How do you know Larry Barnhill?" Devlin asked him.

"He's my cousin."

"And how do you know Edwin Bradley?"

"He's my cousin too."

"And how would you describe the nature of your associations with these two cousins?"

Swan didn't much feel like talking about the strip clubs. "I see 'em at the family reunions," he said. This brought chuckles from the jury, but Swan became serious when questions came up about any role he might have played in the robberies. "I'll take a lie detector test," he declared.

On his way out of the courthouse that evening, he went to step into an elevator, but it was crowded with some of the grand jury members. He figured he'd take the next one, but as the doors closed, he heard one of the members say to another, "He seems like a nice young man." Swan breathed a little easier after that.

Despite the lack of additional information that could help the FBI, Jeff Holmes's testimony at the grand jury hearing—relating again the evidence from Taylor's confession—made the superseding indictment a foregone conclusion. Dwight Thomas had advised waiting for the superseding indictment, and soon we had it. And he and I both knew I stood no chance in a trial. It was time to make a deal. Dwight approached prosecutor Thomas Devlin asking what he could do for me. For an acceptable plea deal, Devlin could be spared the time and expense of a lengthy trial.

But Devlin was playing hardball. "Sorry," he told Dwight. "Unless he knows who the Zodiac murderer was or who killed Tupac, we don't need him. I don't even need him to plead guilty to any other robberies besides the Lilburn First Union. We don't even need *that* robbery. We have him on discharging a weapon at law enforcement officers. Twenty-five years per count. Not to mention carjacking. Your client has enough going against him that we could put him away forever."

Dwight explained Devlin's position to me. "You gotta understand, Larry," he said, "you've pissed a lot of people off. This is big. Really big. The FBI has been stymied for ten years. You made 'em look bad, and they'd love to see you guys rot in prison. Not to mention how pissed off the entire banking industry is. These are some powerful folks, and they're not feeling very forgiving. And, Larry, there's something else. Look at the indictment. You see who the plaintiff is in this case? It's not First Union bank. It's not the police department of Lilburn, Georgia. It's *the United States of America*. You think the damn government is not going to get its way? But look, here's what's in your favor: Until now you've got a spotless record. Maybe your background will influence the judge to show you some leniency."

Meanwhile, Cannon and Bradley had their own attorneys. Dwight was talking to them all, and the group was going back and forth with Devlin. All parties finally agreed: we'd plead guilty to the Lilburn robbery and accept a twenty-six-year sentence. But I knew the judge had some discretion, and I clung to Dwight's words; maybe she'd show some leniency. Maybe she'd cut the twenty-six in half. Maybe I could be out in thirteen years. Maybe even ten or eleven.

Until the sentencing hearing, I was released into the general prison population. I was no longer isolated, but the upgrade was not without its problems. Prisons aren't filled with the best people. I got into two fights. The first almost right away, the result of anger I was harboring inside that I didn't even know was there. In the rec yard, a guard discovered that someone had taken his pen. Pens were a hot commodity as the prisoners would often use the ink to make tattoos. There were ten of us out there, as prisoners were taken out to the yard and brought back in by groups of ten.

"Okay, ain't no one going nowhere," the guard said, "until I get my pen back." When nobody said anything, he added, "Guess maybe we'll have to strip-search y'all when we get inside." Someone, unseen, dropped the pen to the ground and the guard picked it up and that was the last of it, or so I thought. But then one of the other prisoners decided to test me. I was new, after all. He pointed at me and said, "Bet it was that dude told the guard someone took the pen. He looks like a rat."

I knew I had to respond. "When we get back to the pod, I'm going to show you what a rat is," I said. When they took us back and left us to return to our rooms, I unloaded on him. Everything I'd been feeling inside came out all at once. They tried to pull us apart, but I couldn't stop. He went down with my final punch to his head, but I broke my hand in the process. Afterward they took me to the hospital while I tried to process my actions, shocked at the fury I had unleashed.

But not sorry. From that time onward, the Morning Glory boys were respected as more than bank robbers. We weren't to be fucked with. Still, I had one more fight. Sometimes we'd play spades for things like sodas or chips or honey buns. When I'd win, I'd give the winnings to others in the pod. I didn't need it; I was just playing to pass the time. One prisoner considered it arrogant, and maybe it looked that way, with me giving handouts like I was some fucking humanitarian. The dude was a six-foot-four, 230-pound brother, and after one game in which my partner and I beat him and his partner and I once again gave away my winnings, he cold-cocked me. To make the fight more fair, I grabbed a chair and broke it over his back. The fight was quickly broken up, but it was clear by then that I wasn't one to back down. But I learned a lesson about gambling in prison that day: not to do it. I could have been killed over a fucking honey bun.

Sentencing day finally came, and it was back in front of Judge Orinda Evans. Devlin lined up seemingly every bank employee who'd been present during our robberies to give victim impact statements, each one telling of the harrowing ordeal they'd experienced. There were so many of them that the judge interrupted at one point to say that she had read the investigative reports carefully and was well aware of the events in question. Perhaps not everyone had to speak. But Devlin insisted and, by Geogia law, each witness got their turn. For three hours, one by one, the victims of the Morning Glory Gang related the terror they had felt, the fear for their lives. Some had had recurring nightmares of armed men pointing guns in their faces. I was stunned by the accounts, and ashamed that I had never really thought about how our actions had affected these good people.

The defense had its opportunity to make an impression on the judge too. We could put people on the stand to speak on our behalf, to testify to our character. Friends and family took the stand, everyone saying how shocked they were. The bank robberies were "out of character." They were not "representative" of who we really were. The minister of our church talked about my work in securing sponsorships to pay for new choir robes, but I think he was there mainly in support of Regina's family, longtime members. Kevin took the stand too. I'd seen him in the hallway beforehand and we'd exchanged awkward half smiles. He'd come to see me not long after the arrest, and I'd told him things were going to be okay, that I wasn't really *that* involved. By the sentencing hearing, he knew better. Like everyone else, he took the stand with feelings of anger and betrayal. It was a hellish type of humiliation to sit and listen to people trying their best to say good things about me—a man who'd been living a criminal life they'd had no idea about.

Finally, Judge Evans pronounced sentence. It wasn't going to be ten years as I'd hoped. Or eleven. Or thirteen. There would be no leniency, no mitigation because of a clean record. Judge Evans gave the full amount. Three-hundred and twelve months. I wasn't going to see the outside world for twenty-six years.

21

10,000 Days

When Judge Evans passed sentence, she explained that she had very little room to deviate from what the prosecutor had asked for. Too lenient a sentence would almost certainly have triggered an appeal by Devlin. "Even in the case of Mr. Barnhill, here before me," she said, noting not only my clean record but also my career accomplishments.

She'd sentenced bank robbers before, Evans told the courtroom, but never anybody like me. And that's when it struck me that in her eyes, in the eyes of the law, I was no different than those other bank robbers. Devlin had purposely grouped all four of us together in the plea deal to emphasize that point. There could be no special cases. My clean record didn't matter. My university degree didn't matter. My life as a successful businessman didn't matter. And none of what my supporters said on the stand could make a difference either. When I joined the Morning Glory Boys, I became one of them. Who was I? I was a gangster. I was a criminal. That's who I was. That's who I had chosen to be.

There were differences in our sentences, but they were because of decisions we made after our arrest. Bradley and I got twenty-six years. Cannon decided at the last minute to back out of the plea. He was ready to take his chances with a jury. But then he got cold feet and changed his mind. Devlin made him pay for that. Hard. The plea for Cannon rose from twenty-six years to thirty-four, and that's what Judge Evans gave him. Taylor, for breaking the pledge we'd all made and cooperating, got no more than five years shaved off his sentence. He'd still have to serve twenty-one years in prison.

After the sentencing, it was back to ACDC. All the inmates there had heard the news. The TV news stations had been blaring it all afternoon: "The members of the Morning Glory Boys, who have terrorized Atlanta for more than a decade, were sentenced today to over one hundred years in total." When I walked into the pod, everyone's head turned toward me, and the place became quiet as a church. I went into my room and climbed up into my bed.

At four in the morning, a guard came to escort me to a holding cell. It had been decided that until our transport to the federal penitentiaries that we were all eventually bound for, it would be better if we were out of the mainstream prison population and sent somewhere quieter. We were going to be transferred to a county jail away from Atlanta. Bradley and Cannon and Taylor all came into the holding area, each escorted separately. Nobody said a word.

Someone else was in the prison sally port too, and you could tell it was someone important by the extra level of security that was in place that morning. H. Rap Brown was a Muslim cleric and Black separatist. At one point, back in the 1960s, he'd been the Black Panthers' minister of justice. He'd served time before. In the '70s he spent a few years in Attica, where he converted to Islam and changed his name to Jamil Abdullah al-Amin. When he got out he moved to Atlanta's West End, where he opened a grocery store and lived as a Muslim spiritual leader. Cannon's gun had come from the West End, from the Muslim neighborhood where Yusuf had his shop. Yusuf, who had lied to the FBI for us. The police weren't popular there, and guys like al-Amin weren't popular with the police. Al-Amin hadn't lost his separatist views or given up on his radical activism. Just a couple of months after our arrest, two sheriff's deputies tried to serve him with a warrant for some outstanding charge, and he allegedly gunned them both down. Then he fled for Alabama, where US marshals found him after a four-day manhunt. His next stop was ACDC.

Now al-Amin was waiting just like us to be transferred somewhere else, though I had no idea where he was heading.

Somehow, his presence there that morning opened my eyes. I'd been rendered more or less numb when Judge Orinda Evans had pronounced my sentence the day before. But now it hit me: This shit was real. I was sharing space with an alleged cop killer. This was now where I belonged. *Who was I? I was a gangster. I was a criminal.*

We spent three weeks in the county jail. It was in a more rural area of Georgia, and the white guards were all good ol' boys, but they treated us okay. I spent the time coming to grips with my new reality, finally deciding that I needed to man up and do the time. I couldn't lay down and die. I was a fighter, wasn't I? So I had to fight. I had to face what I had to face and survive.

From the county jail, we were split up. I went to United States Penitentiary Atlanta for five months, and then on to what would become my home for the foreseeable future: the Federal Correctional Institute, Otisville, a federal prison in the southern part of New York State. It was a couple hours' drive from New York City, but because I wouldn't be seeing the outside of it, it really didn't matter to me where it was.

The funny thing about being in prison is that you have a lot of time to think about all the people you left on the outside. I let a lot of people down, and every one of them passed through my mind as I wondered what they thought of me now. I knew my marriage was over. Before being sent to

Otisville, I'd had a chance to talk to Regina. I told her that I knew she had to get on with her life. It sure as hell wasn't like she needed my permission, but I thought it was important that she hear me say it.

I thought about my son. I thought about my mother. And I thought about three young men I had been mentoring as a member of 100 Black Men of South Florida, a nonprofit group of men in business and government organized to mentor Black Americans and other minorities, typically at-risk young people. One of the young men lived in Carol City, one lived in Liberty City, and one lived in Brownsville, also known as Brown Sub. None of these Miami neighborhoods were what you'd call high end. These kids all came from broken homes with no solid male role models. I tried to be that for them. I tried to show them what a Black man could do in America. I took them to sporting and other events, and we'd talk about their futures. I wanted to teach them a different way to live than what they saw in the neighborhoods they came from. You didn't need to sell drugs. You didn't need to join a gang. You didn't need to live a life outside the law. You could succeed in life just like I had.

Just like I had. I couldn't even imagine what went through their minds the day they found out their mentor was a bank robber, a member of a criminal gang, a man who'd worn a mask and pointed a gun at innocent bank employees. I didn't hear from them or see them after the arrest. They didn't come to the sentencing hearing. They didn't visit me. Why would they? All I'd done was lie to them. In fact, I would never see any of these young men again.

I thought about *everybody*. I thought about people I hadn't seen in years. I thought about childhood friends. I thought about college classmates. I thought about girlfriends. I thought about people I knew from church. I thought about people I'd met in Memphis and New Orleans. People I'd completely forgotten about would pop into my head. With every one of them, I thought the same thing: what will they think when they learn of what happened to Larry Barnhill?

Some people stuck by me. Most did not. I knew I could never blame those who abandoned me. After all, I'd abandoned them first. I abandoned them the day I decided to abandon the rules of civilized society. From that point on, I had no right to demand or expect any kind of loyalty or friendship from anyone. I forfeited those rights when I joined the Morning Glory Gang.

Otisville held about a thousand prisoners. What struck me about the place was how self-contained it was. Sure, you expect that of a prison. But it wasn't just that it was isolated from the rest of the world; it was that it *resembled*, in some way, the rest of the world. It was a city in and of itself. An entire society behind a fence, with a hierarchy and political structure. I guess every community has its structure, even prison communities. You learn quickly who's who. Whom you can trust, whom you can't. Whom you go to for what. You learn who's a member of a white supremacist gang, who's a member of a militant Black gang, who's a member of a Latino or Mexican gang. Who's running drugs. Who's running gambling. Who's running the recreation. Who's running the food. Which TV room is tuned to Fox, which TV room is tuned to CNN.

They give you a handbook when you go in, but this political hierarchy, this community structure, isn't discussed. The handbook tells you about practical matters like the inmate counts. Counts take place at midnight, 3 a.m., 5 a.m., 4 p.m., and 10 p.m. The last two are stand-up counts and entail what the name implies: you drop whatever you're doing, and you stand in your cell until you've been officially counted. You learn about the meals and that they are served daily in Food Service, where it is expected you will be dressed appropriately—the khaki shirt you were issued when you entered Otisville tucked into your khaki pants, proper undergarments, and approved footwear (no shower shoes, the handbook reminds you).

You are told you have the right to be safe from sexually abusive behavior, and the handbook lists some suggestions to prevent same, including carrying yourself "in a confident manner at all times." It advises you not to "permit your emotions (fear/anxiety) to be obvious to others." It is highly recommended that you never accept gifts or favors. "Most gifts or favors come with strings attached to them." Other suggestions: "Choose your associates wisely," and "Be alert!"

There is a list of conduct codes in the handbook starting at code 100 and running up to code 499. The highest codes are for the least egregious offenses, and as the numbers get lower, the offenses are more serious. A 404 is "using abusive or obscene language." A 332 is "smoking where prohibited," and a 300 is "indecent exposure." A 219 is stealing and a 201 is fighting. A 105 is rioting. Code 100 is murder.

Finally, the daily schedule is listed:

6:00 a.m.: Wake-up call / Lights on

6:15 a.m.: Breakfast

7:15–7:30 a.m.: Sick call

7:30 a.m.: Work call

7:30–10:00 a.m.: Unit sanitation

8:30–10:45 a.m.: Leisure time activities (if unit sanitation is acceptable).

10:45 a.m.–12:30 p.m.: Lunch

12:30–3:00 p.m.: Unit sanitation

12:30–3:30 p.m.: Work call

4:00 p.m.: Stand-up count

4:30–6:00 p.m.: Dinner

CONTROL. MOVE. DOMINATE.

5:00–8:45 p.m.: Leisure time

10:00 p.m.: Stand-up count

11:30 p.m.: Lights off

As I read that schedule in my handbook the day after I arrived, it dawned on me how bare and simple my life had become. Everything that had given me any kind of meaning or enjoyment or gratification had been stripped away, and this was all that was now left. The daily schedule would represent the next twenty-six years of my life. Every single day would be like this. And I did the math: there would be close to 10,000 of them.

22

KILLING TIME

Federal prisons don't look like they do in old movies. You don't get escorted into a cold cell of steel bars. The cells aren't really cells at all. They're more like dorm rooms. Semi-comfortable bunks, wooden desks, toilet, sink, decent lighting.

You also have some discretion over which room you end up in and what roommate you'll have. You start in a common area with maybe a dozen other guys. You get to know the others in the common area, you find someone you think you're most compatible with, and you barter for a room. I found a room I liked and offered the occupants a certain amount of money for it. They agreed to move temporarily back to the common area while my chosen roommate and I moved into their room. In time they found another room. Of course the moves have to be cleared by the floor officer, and everyone knows that money changes hands, but it's an effective system. Black inmates don't end up living with, or next to, members of the Aryan Nations, and a straight guy doesn't have to worry about being incarcerated with a gay man.

My roommate had been a big-time party promoter in New York. He knew a lot of people and had even dated Madonna at one point. But he'd been busted for conspiracy, attempted distribution of cocaine, and illegal gun possession. The room we chose was next door to a member of the Colombo crime family. In fact, there were a few members of organized crime in Otisville at the time. Early on, some of the mobsters actually mentored me on the dynamics of the prison. These Italian guys weren't necessarily known for their love of Black people, but they learned of my background with the Orange Bowl and my business success, and they saw how I carried myself. They came from money, and I had been around money. Lots of money. They knew I was no stranger to the streets, which they respected, but they also knew I was no street thug, which they respected even more.

There were other high-profile inmates in Otisville, including George Jung, a.k.a. Boston George. In Colombia, he was known simply as El Americano. George smuggled cocaine for the Medellin Cartel, headed by Pablo Escobar, in the 1970s and 1980s. He was imprisoned in 1994 for sixty years but would be released in 2014 after testifying against Carlos Lehder, his ex-partner. Johnny Depp played Boston George in the biopic *Blow* in 2001, making George not just high profile in Otisville but a bona fide celebrity.

It didn't take me long to get acclimated to my new home. The schedule mentions "work call" and that's not optional. Unless you're medically unable, you're put to work in the warehouse, or as a groundskeeper, or a painter, or a plumber, or a food service worker. Or maybe as an inmate orderly. Hourly pay is typically somewhere between twelve cents and forty cents. This goes into your commissary account, which you can use to buy snacks, postage stamps, paper, underwear, soda, and even small electronic items like radios, calculators, and clocks.

I worked in the commissary, but I also asked to do another kind of work that I had thought about all the way back in ACDC. I saw right away who the prototypical inmate was: young, Black, no high school education, coming from a poor neighborhood, no decent role models, and probably convicted of some kind of minor drug or weapons charge. What was the future for a kid like that? They had no direction, no one to point the way. I knew I couldn't mentor those three young men from Miami anymore, but maybe I could mentor the young men I was in prison with. There were hundreds of them, after all. I asked to work in the education department, and I became a GED instructor.

Then I spent my energy trying to drive some of these kids into my class. "What are you going to do when you get out," I'd ask them, "without a high school degree?" I'd tell them to learn a trade, to work their way up from whatever shitty job they were doing at the prison. I'd tell them to get their GED, emphasizing that they'd go nowhere without it once they hit the outside. Their lives could be better. There were other ways to live than the ways they knew of, the ways we *both* knew of. "Sure, maybe the system is stacked against you," I'd say, "but fuck the system. More importantly, fuck the idea that you can't compete, that you can't make it. With the right tools, you can overcome it all."

Some of these young men couldn't even read, so I would start there. Some of them were fathers. "You want to be able to read to your child, right?" I would ask. "When your kid sends you a letter, don't you want to be able to read it yourself, instead of having to hand it to someone else to read it for you? Don't you want to be able to help them with their homework some day? Look, if you don't want to learn to read for yourself, do it for your child."

The key was finding the right thread. It wasn't enough to tell someone who's probably never seen more than a hundred bucks in their life what was right and what was wrong. I had to find the common ground, the thread that could tie it all together for them. And I'd assure them I'd be right there with them. "I'll be teaching the GED class," I'd say. "I'll see you through it." For some of these kids, I might have been the first person besides their mothers to ever show any concern for their futures.

I started working on something else in Otisville too. I knew the story of the Morning Glory Boys wasn't going to go away with time. It was a compelling narrative. Until our arrest, we were generally regarded as the most successful bank robbers in US history. That would have been an interesting story in and of itself, but to my mind, the real story was what got us there. Or at least what got *me* there. I wouldn't presume to speak for the others. For me, I felt as if a story about greed might be valuable. About wanting it all, without realizing what *all* even means. About wanting more, about feeding an insatiable appetite, about putting yourself on a treadmill to absolutely fucking nowhere. And doing so with no regard for others. I knew I could never legally profit from the story, but if I could help even one young kid, or high school student, or college student, or young professional who was thinking of embarking on a gangster life of crime—well, that would be profit enough for me. And so I began to think about writing my story.

My roommate encouraged me. In time, he would write his own book about all the celebrities he'd dealt with in his party-promotion business. He told me about *Don Diva* magazine, a publication written for prison inmates that did feature stories on high-profile criminals. A husband and wife had started the magazine, which bills itself as the "Original Street Bible," in 1999, presumably as a way to give inmates a voice. He thought my story was tailor-made for *Don Diva*. But in the common area, Boston George overheard us and approached me later. "Larry," he said, "don't give your story to them. Your story is bigger than that. Listen, let me get you in touch with Bruce Porter." As it happened, Porter wrote the screenplay for *Blow*. Not only that, he'd written the book that the movie was based on, a *New York Times* bestseller.

I spoke by phone to Bruce not long afterward. He was interested. He wanted me to work with Boston George to write a manuscript, and then he'd take a look at it. I would write, George would edit, and then we'd have another inmate type it up. But in the midst of the work, I was transferred to Federal Correctional Institution, Cumberland, a medium-security prison in a rural area of Maryland. It was 2002. I was now two years into my sentence.

Without George's help, I worked on the manuscript only now and then. I mostly kept my head down, did my work, and got along as best I could. The manuscript idea more or less faded into the background and, somehow, another two years went by. In 2004, I was sent to FCI, Fort Dix, a low-security facility in New Jersey. That's the way you proceed through prison. You move from higher-security institutions to progressively lower-security facilities, assuming, of course, that you're following all the rules.

At Fort Dix, I met another mob member. His father was the boss of a big crime family until his death in 2005. The son and I would work out together every morning. I didn't ask a lot of questions about his past, and he didn't ask a lot about mine. It's not like I had any right to judge the man. I was a convicted criminal too.

And then came another transferee. Improbably, Boston George was sent to Fort Dix. We were back together, and we started up on the manuscript again. Eventually, we finished it and George sent it to Bruce Porter. Porter sent it to a young director in LA by the name of Thomas Durant. In the meantime, I sent the manuscript to my cousin Swan. Besides the car business, Swan had some inroads with the music industry. He knew a producer named DJ Toomp who put the manuscript into the hands of an Atlanta-raised producer who remembered the news accounts of the bank heists, and he, in turn, put Swan in touch with a screenwriter, Siddeeqah "Sid" Powell, who had written some screenplays for a few successful TV movies. Sid came to visit me and worked on another script, but the logistics and timing just weren't right and we couldn't seem to get it together. Boston George and

I waited to hear something from LA, but nothing seemed to materialize.

I stayed in Fort Dix until 2006. Then I was sent to FCI Coleman in Florida, about an hour's drive northwest of Orlando. Another low-security place, Coleman would become my home for the next eleven years.

23

A NUMBER

There were about fifteen-hundred inmates at Coleman in four facilities. As in the previous places, I worked at the commissary, a huge operation. Each facility at Coleman had a commissary, each one like a grocery store, and there was an extensive warehouse too. The whole Coleman complex handled more than $10 million worth of inventory a year. I worked as a clerk and did all the ordering for every item sold in my facility's store. I ordered from places like Keefe Supply Company, a leading supplier of food and personal care items to commissaries around the country, and other wholesalers like Mister Snacks. I had other inmates working with me, doing the receiving and the stocking. For prison, it was a pretty decent gig and a good way to spend eight hours a day. Keeping busy made the days go by faster.

The commissary was under the control of the Bureau of Prisons, and my superiors were civilian officers. One was a Hispanic man who didn't like me at all. Vázquez was a local, the product of rural Florida, and he was racist. He didn't have my education, and it bothered him that a Black man could be as educated as I was, while he, of Cuban descent, somehow never got the same opportunities. He called me privileged one day.

"Privileged?" I said. "I'm doing twenty-six years, Vázquez. You get to go home every night. What the fuck you mean 'privileged'?"

The commissary organization rotated its civilian employees around the four facilities every quarter. Whenever it was Vázquez's turn at our facility, he'd get someone else to do my job and I'd be out. Other prison officials couldn't understand it. Even the warden knew I was the best, most experienced man for the job, but the commissary was its own entity and the warden wouldn't interfere. Besides, no matter what he thought, he would never support a convict over a civilian. Fortunately, another supervisor, Mr. Thompson, who ran the rec yard, would hire me for that quarter. I would sweep and clean up and do whatever odd jobs the rec yard required. The job fulfilled the inmate requirement, but it didn't pay nearly as much. I made $240 a month as the clerk in the commissary and only $34 in the rec yard. But soon enough, the quarter would end, Vázquez would move on to the next facility in the rotation, and I'd get my clerk position back.

Mr. Thompson was a good man. And I had other supervisors who were good men too, like Mr. Collins and Mr. Adams. These men would mentor me and help me keep my head straight. Early on, especially, it was hard. When you're facing almost three decades in prison, time stretches on ahead of you forever. There were times I imagined I was going to die in prison. That I'd never see the light of day. I'd either be the victim of another inmate in a fight gone terribly wrong or the victim of the prison system's less-than-stellar health care. Through the angst and frustration, these men helped me stay sane.

I also learned that it can often be a matter of perspective. Everything is relative. I would talk to lifers who would say, "Twenty-six years? Sure, maybe that's a long time, but it's a damn number, Barnhill. You got yourself *a number*." Even guys who had big numbers—forty or fifty years, even seventy or eighty—had hope. They could hope for a change in the sentencing laws, which happened on occasion. The lifers had no such hope. Sure, there are always stories of new evidence coming in on a case that results in a new trial or even complete exoneration, but those stories are rare. Most of the lifers I met had come to accept that they were going to die in prison.

I knew something else. There was something called "good time." Assuming I followed all the rules, I'd have to serve only 85 percent of my sentence. Good time, or good-time credit, or gain time, as it's alternatively called, kicks in automatically, meaning twenty-six years would be shaved to twenty-two. That might not seem like much, but think about four more years in a federal penitentiary versus four years of freedom. Believe me, it's a lot.

There were a few people who stuck by me and came to visit on a regular basis. One of those people was Donna, the woman I had met years before in Miami, the woman I had dated but who saw my lifestyle in Atlanta and had said to me, "Somewhere along the line, you're going to have to figure out what's really important to you." Our romantic relationship ended that day, but we'd kept in touch regularly. Donna found out about the arrest from a mutual friend, and she'd been just as shocked as anyone. Then she came to Atlanta to visit me at ACDC, and she never stopped visiting me since. Two or three times a year, she'd come see me. Didn't matter where—Otisville, Cumberland, Fort Dix, Coleman.

Others stuck by me too. Mom visited a couple of times a year, at least. Dad would visit me in Fort Dix, but he didn't like to fly, so once I was moved to Coleman, our visits were strictly over the phone. My cousin Swan came to see me often. So did Rachel and Kenny, my longtime friends from Miami. We'd partied like rock stars back then. After I'd landed in Coleman, they both visited me at least once every other month. Loyal then, loyal now.

At first, my son would come see me with his mother, but as he got older, the visits became less and less frequent. Finally, he stopped coming altogether. He had his own life to live, plus he resented the fact that by my own actions, I was no longer there for him. For my part, I needed him; I needed to see him, to talk to him, to try as best I could to still be involved in his life. But I understood.

Meanwhile, the film idea that had been born back at Otisville hadn't completely died. As it happened, Swan had given my manuscript to an actor and writer who had come to him from a producer he'd met. Swan was meeting a lot of people, and it seemed like interest in my story was picking up. The writer came to see me, and then we talked through a series of phone calls and the prison email system. Like Sid, the writer put a script together and that script he, the producer, and Swan took to the annual American Film Market event in Los Angeles. There, the script grabbed the attention of Jerome Martin, manager of Tyrese, an actor and R&B singer who'd become famous in the *Fast & Furious* movies. Jerome could see Tyrese playing me.

The problem with all this was that I was incarcerated. There was a lot of activity, a lot of talk, and a lot of interest. Over time, since Otisville, in fact, scripts had been written, contacts had been drafted, conversations—even negotiations—had taken place. But I began to think that nothing was really going to happen because the one man who could make certain that a deal would come to fruition, that all the talk would become something solid, was unavailable. That man was me. From where I was sitting, I could only watch.

And then fate intervened. Tyrese and his manager, Jerome Martin, happened to attend a Floyd Mayweather fight. At the fight, they ran into an acquaintance whom I knew well: Skip Davis. Skip, of course, was a contact of mine from back in my Miami Arena days. He was with Haymon Entertainment, and he'd brought some huge names into the venue. We'd become close friends. Skip knew everybody, but I hadn't thought of involving Skip initially in the film project because I knew Hayman Entertainment had shifted its focus to the boxing business. In fact, it was Hayman who'd put the Mayweather fight together. Al Hayman had become one of the biggest promoters, if not the biggest, in the country.

And there was another reason. I hadn't talked to Skip since the arrest. Sure, we'd been close friends, but what did he think of me now? I found out soon enough. That night, Tyrese and Jerome offhandedly mentioned to Skip the story about a bank robber, a story they saw as a good potential film project. The robber, they told Skip, was in the arena concert industry and his name was Larry Barnhill. Skip's jaw dropped. A couple of days later, Skip called Donna to find out how to get a hold of me, and shortly after that we were talking over the prison phone.

"You're trying to do a movie and you're not involving Hayman Entertainment?" he said.

"Skip, I'm sorry, I didn't know if you'd be interested."

"Interested? Larry, man, you're my brother."

And then we spent an hour or so getting caught up. It took all afternoon. The prison allowed calls of only fifteen minutes, and you had to wait thirty minutes between calls. But it was great talking to Skip. And he wanted to do the film. If there was anyone who could get it off the ground, it was Skip. He took it to Al Hayman, who gave it his blessing, and from that point on Skip and I spoke on the phone every Tuesday to work on a script. Skip traveled a lot for business, but he never missed a call. No matter where he was or what he was doing, if it was Tuesday, we talked. And I knew that Skip's interest in the film was fueled as much by our friendship as by the film's commercial viability. That's the way he was. Later I would hear someone describe how rare a presence Skip was in the entertainment field: It's an industry where everybody is disliked by someone. But not Skip. Nobody ever had a bad thing to say about Skip Davis.

During one of our conversations, Skip shared some distressing news with me. He had cancer, and the prognosis wasn't good. Over the next few months, he received chemo treatments, but the process weakened him to the point where one day he had a heart attack. He underwent heart surgery, but we talked by phone the day after. "I'm doin' good, Larry," he said. "I'm gonna make it." We talked a bit more, then Skip said he needed to rest. "I love you, man," he said before hanging up. Skip always said that, but I sensed something was different this time. He'd told me he was doing good, but I had a bad feeling I couldn't shake.

My friend Skip Davis died the next day.

Al Hayman had given Skip total autonomy to develop the movie idea, and he'd been waiting for Skip to present it to him. Now there would be nothing to present. Without Skip, the idea stalled. Swan and I talked about maybe shifting gears. "Cuz, you could get back to writing the book," he said. "Forget the movie. Publish your memoirs."

Yeah, maybe, I thought. And then I put the idea away for later.

All this time, the days and weeks and years of my incarceration were passing slowly by. At one point I looked ahead and saw not twenty-two years but fifteen. And then ten. And then five. And then two.

With two years left, I was transferred to FCI Jesup, in Georgia, about an hour from Savannah. It was Christmas time. Right after I arrived, I got word that my dad had passed away. We had talked regularly on the phone, but it made me sad to think that the last time I'd actually seen him was when I was at Fort Dix. More than a decade had passed.

With two years left, you start worrying about screwing it up. Some of the lifers would tell me, "Barnhill, you gotta be careful. Anything that could get you into some kind of trouble now—man, you gotta back away from that shit." I took their advice. I even stopped playing basketball for fear that a fight might break out on the court. And then I waited as two years became one, and one year became six months, and six months became two weeks.

With two weeks left, they put me in solitary, except it wasn't solitary. It was quarantine. There was some virus going around. Apparently, it had started in China and before long it had spread all over the planet. I wouldn't have picked the time of COVID to be released out into the world, but I sure as hell wasn't going to argue about it.

The day of my release, the prison made arrangements for an officer to drive me to the Savannah airport, where Swan was going to meet me. We were going to fly to Philly, and from there to Wilmington, where my mother and the rest of my family would be awaiting my return—twenty-two years after my incarceration.

By habit, I slid into the back seat of the prison van. "No, no," the officer said. "Sit up front. In the passenger seat."

"Yeah?"

"Yeah. You're a free man now, Mr. Barnhill."

I nodded and smiled. Free man. It was the best thing anybody had ever called me in my whole life.

24

Acclimating

It wasn't entirely accurate to call me a free man because I wasn't entirely free. I had a year left on my sentence. But because of the length of time I'd already spent in prison and because of my spotless disciplinary record, I'd be serving that year in a halfway house instead of a federal penitentiary. Instead of being behind a fence in FCI Jesup, I'd be in a residence in Wilmington, Delaware, free to come and go (with permission) and close to family.

But to get there, I needed to fly from Savannah. I hadn't flown in an airplane as a commercial passenger for well over twenty years. Before 9/11. Swan was flying in from Atlanta to accompany me to Wilmington, but he couldn't leave the secure part of the airport to guide me through the TSA checkpoints. The van dropped me off at curbside, and I walked into the airport and tried to make sense of all the new procedures. It would have been overwhelming for anybody who hadn't flown commercially in two decades, especially during

COVID. For a person who hadn't been out in the real world in all that time, it was staggering. Quickly, I decided I needed to find a TSA agent to ask for help.

To anyone else in the airport, I'm sure I looked like a regular civilian. I was wearing the street clothes that my family had sent me when I still had a couple of weeks left at Jesup and was carrying a small duffel bag that held all my worldly possessions. It wasn't lost on me that it was the same kind of duffel bag I'd used twenty-five years before to carry stolen bank money. In my wallet I had a debit card the penitentiary had issued to me in the amount of what I had left on my commissary account and $250 in cash, the amount every prisoner is given upon release. The one thing that really separated me from the rest of the airline passengers that day was my prison ID. Of course I hadn't had a driver's license since the arrest. I also had a paper that would tell any law enforcement official, including any TSA official, where I was headed and why.

I spotted a TSA agent, showed him my ID and paper, and asked him for a little help navigating the airport. The man couldn't have been nicer or more understanding. He walked me to security, instructed me on all the intricacies—removing my belt, shoes, and so forth—and wished me luck. The other TSA agents at the security checkpoint said the same thing. One of them even said, "Welcome back."

Once through security, I saw Swan waiting for me in the concourse and breathed a sigh of relief. Now I had someone to guide me through my first day on the outside. We flew from Savannah to Charlotte, and from Charlotte to Philly. My sister and brother were there to greet me, and then we drove on to Wilmington. Everything seemed to move so fast. I wanted to slow down and look at the scenery around me, but for the whole day, from the prison van until Wilmington, I felt like I couldn't keep up with the pace of this new world. Everything looked familiar, but everything looked different.

I sure as hell wasn't used to the food. My sister had a fresh Italian sub waiting for me in the car. Best thing I'd eaten in twenty years. Problem was, I couldn't keep it down. Lesson learned: I'd have to ease my system back into the cuisine of the outside world. The incident acted as a fitting metaphor for everything about my new life. In front of me there would be a lot of acclimating. In 2000, iPhones didn't exist. Most computers were still on dial-up. Amazon was fairly new, and Wikipedia hadn't been born yet. Facebook was still in the future. So was Gmail, streaming, and going anywhere by Uber. I had a lot of catching up to do.

On the way to the halfway house, we swung by my mother's house, where she could lay eyes on the son she hadn't seen in so, so long. Then it was off to my home for the next twelve months, a twenty-eight-room house with about a dozen recently released men just like myself, all trying to start their lives over. We had our own rooms, which was a welcome change, and meals were included. Good meals too, but if you didn't like what they served, you were welcome to use the kitchen to cook your own food. My sister Terry stopped by often with takeout, or maybe a plate of something she'd cooked over the weekend.

There were five or six employees there, including a case manager and an employment specialist. There were no guards. There was no reason to escape, after all. These people were there to provide guidance, help us find jobs, get us access to health care, and steer us back into society.

I had additional help. There were some beautiful people who knew me from way back and were glad to see me return to Wilmington, even with the baggage I carried. James Ray Rhodes was one of those people. When we were kids, we lived a block apart, and we practically grew up together. We became especially close through the Boys Club. We both wanted to be architects back in those days and wanted to go to big universities after high school. While I went to Florida, Ray went off to Ohio State. He spent a year there before enlisting in the military to help finance his schooling. We didn't see much of each other after that, but we always kept in touch. And when I went to prison, Ray wrote to me regularly, always asking how I was getting along. He never once asked about the bank robberies, the Morning Glory Gang, or what had happened to me to put me on my criminal path. He cared only about how I was doing.

Ray went on to have a fine career. He left the military, got his architecture degree from Hampton University, and then held a series of successful positions. By the time I got out, he was a pillar of the community and executive director of the Christina Cultural Arts Center, a program in Wilmington with a mission to use arts education to promote school success, career training, and positive social behavior. Ray started helping me almost immediately, picking me up at the halfway house and driving me to job fairs and interviews. He'd offer recommendations, putting his own hard-earned reputation on the line. "What do you need, Larry?" he would ask me. "Let's get you moving forward. Just let me know what you need."

Another man in my corner was Jeff Starkey, who had been a senior at Howard Career Center when I had transferred there from Glasgow High. Like Ray, Jeff had gone to Hampton University, and we'd kept in touch over the years. In fact, Jeff happened to be in Atlanta three months before my arrest, and we'd had a drink together. Like everyone else, he was stunned when he heard the news three months later.

Jeff was now commissioner for the Department of Public Works in Wilmington and he, too, was willing to put his reputation on the line for me. He was instrumental in introducing me to the right people, telling me that he knew how sincere I was in putting my life back together. "Larry," he'd tell me, "I know I don't have to worry about you. There are other people you and I grew up with who have gotten themselves incarcerated, and I can tell who's heading back. You're not one of them. That's not the way you're built."

Jeff's best advice was to remind me to slow down. After two decades in prison, I wanted to get caught up all at once. I had to make up for lost time. Other people my age were winding down their careers, and I felt like I was just starting out. Jeff could sense my impatience. "You can't rush it, Larry," he would say. "One step at a time."

Steve Washington was another childhood friend. In fact, Steve, Jeff, Ray, and I had all hung out together back at the Boys Club so many years before. Steve had gone on to become a teacher. He wasn't unfamiliar with the justice system; in fact, he served as a board member on the State of Delaware Board of Parole. He'd seen his share of criminals but never regarded me as one. When I returned to Wilmington, Steve didn't once ask me about my past. To him I was an old friend from the Jackson Street Boys Club, and we picked up right where we'd left off. Like Ray and Jeff, Steve just wanted to help me get on with my life.

My first job was with a groundskeeping crew for the parks and recreation department of the city. We'd do lawn maintenance at all the different parks around town, some of which I remembered from when I was a kid. I ran the blower. To get to my job, I caught a bus at five fifteen every morning. I hadn't ridden a public bus since college. It sure wasn't like putting on a business suit and jumping into my Lexus; those days seemed impossibly long ago. But after twenty-two years in prison, I enjoyed being out every day. The fresh air and sunshine felt good.

My only problem with the job was what I'd hear coming out of the mouths of some of my coworkers. The discussions about women and partying—discussions that used to be normal to me—now made me uncomfortable. I had no right to judge anybody, but my desire to make positive changes in the lives of those around me kept me out of those conversations. I knew I needed to surround myself with positive, uplifting people. I had to find a better job.

25

MOVING FORWARD

While I was working and acclimating to my new life, I was attending reentry court once every other week, which eventually would be reduced to once a month. Reentry court in Delaware provides oversight and assistance for individuals on probation. It's a support system. The other way of doing probation is the punitive approach, and if you choose to take the wrong steps in your reclamation, that's the approach you'll get. Me, I was interested only in doing the right things. I was working on reinventing myself as someone who could influence and support people in underserved communities and those returning to society from prison. I appreciated the support of the reentry program and Judge Christopher Burke, who presided over the reentry court. He could not have been more encouraging. At the hearings, you talk about what you're doing and what kind of path you're on. Judge Burke was always very attentive and interested in what I had to say. I knew this was a man who cared.

Working with those of us in Judge Burke's court was Wes Southall, director of the Community Partner Support Unit (CPSU), an organization that came under the Division of Social Services at the Department of Health and Social Services for the state of Delaware. Wes was the chief administrator for the division, and the CPSU was tasked with providing social services to those who are really in need—the marginalized, the neglected, those well below the poverty line, the so-called TANF population: those benefitting from the Temporary Assistance for Needy Families program.

Wes was in a position to support those in the reentry court with training programs, even jobs. Wes got a hold of my résumé from David Coker, a senior administrator for the department. David had received my resume from Swan, who'd never stopped supporting me. Wes set up an appointment for me to come in and talk to him about a job. He thought I might be able to work with CPSU.

Sitting across from him in his office, I decided I was no longer hiding anything from anybody. I thought it best that we discuss my crimes and incarceration before getting too far into the conversation. I said, "Wes, I don't know if you know about my background—"

Wes cut me off. "Yeah, I googled you," he said, "but it doesn't matter. I'm not going to ask for an explanation, because I think we both know there's really no good one you could offer."

I nodded in return, and that's the last that was said about my past. We chatted some more, and then Wes offered me a job. Later he would tell me that he appreciated my desire to want to give back, to prevent others from making the same mistakes I had made. My role would be to counsel and help those who had recently been released, connecting them with available social services, training, and job opportunities. It was a social services position, so it didn't pay a lot, but it was my first full-time position since prison and it beat the hell out of having a leaf blower strapped to my back. And I did well at it. I could speak to the people who came to us and were trying to restart their lives. I had street cred. I was trying to restart my life too. In addition to hooking them up with opportunities, I did my best to encourage them, give them hope, and make them feel positive about their lives and what was ahead for them.

Besides giving me a job, Wes helped me get up to speed on some of the practical matters of life in the twenty-first century, helping me enroll in computer classes sponsored by Goodwill. Sure, I had some catching up to do, but before long I became fairly proficient. Eventually, I got my driver's license too. I also learned the intricacies of the smartphone. I'd received one that first day at Mom's house and spent time figuring it out, helped a lot by Nikki, an old friend I'd reconnected with.

In the meantime, I was looking for ways to move farther ahead in my new life. One day Ray Rhodes introduced me to a gentleman by the name of Saad Soliman. Saad was a well-known force in the public sector, a man dedicated to advocating for those in need of opportunity and resources. He'd worked for years helping marginalized people, especially people out of prison with no clear plan of how exactly to get back into a productive life.

Here's the interesting thing about Saad: He was one of those people himself at one time. Saad had done time. And when he got out, he learned firsthand of the difficulties of assimilating back into society as a convicted felon. He put that experience to good use and managed to get hired by the United States Department of Justice as a reentry specialist, ultimately overhauling the federal probation office in Wilmington. He'd even helped launch the halfway house I'd been living in.

After talking to Ray, Saad came to see me one day. We talked, and he liked how committed I was to reengaging with the world after having spent so much time in prison. Then he offered me a job at a nonprofit organization where he was executive director. Peace by Piece was founded by Kelli DiSabatino, owner of a local residential treatment home for people with substance use disorder. Peace by Piece was established to reduce barriers for people reentering society by not only helping them find work but also by providing a community for like people, thus creating an environment where we were all helping each other.

I met Kelli, who knew all about the need for opportunities for people looking to restart their lives. "We all make mistakes," she said. "It's not about what we've done; it's about what we're going to do about it. It's about accountability and taking responsibility. And at the end of the day, it's about the legacy that we're leaving behind." But Kelli was realistic. She understood the hurdles that the system puts up—governmental, political, financial. She was trying to make a difference.

She liked my administrative experience, and she liked my attitude. To her I looked like a man ready to "light the world on fire." I started as a case manager, and before too long I became director of operations. It was a great experience.

Then Saad helped me move onto something else. He had connections with the Wilmington Alliance, a nonprofit organization of civic and business leaders that helped create economic opportunities for historically underserved Wilmington communities. Basically, the organization worked with the people of these communities to align resources and fill gaps, providing support where it was needed and removing barriers for small businesses and entrepreneurs and neighborhood revitalization projects. Gregg Bunkley, a community engagement specialist, had insisted I submit my résumé, and I ended up interviewing with Dr. Hara Wright-Smith, director of economic development and inclusion for the Wilmington Alliance.

During the interview, Dr. Wright-Smith told me that the Wilmington Alliance's workforce development arm was looking for help to expand the Second Chance Employment initiative and outside relationships with potential partners for the initiative. Second Chance was designed to help land jobs for nontraditional job seekers, specifically formerly incarcerated individuals. Naturally, I knew more than a little about the circumstances those individuals face when trying to reenter society. The Wilmington Alliance was looking to hire an employer navigator to work with potential employers, mainly to understand their hiring practices and requirements and to determine the workforce needs they might have that could be filled by skilled people seeking, as the name of the initiative implied, a second chance. I had the experience of having been incarcerated, so I could speak the language of the job applicants, and I had the administrative and managerial experience of the business world, so I could speak the language of the potential employers.

I knew how to build relationships too. Dr. Wright-Smith saw that, taking note of the relationships I'd already built in the Wilmington area in my relatively short time out of prison. Hiring me was okay with her, but I needed to talk to others, including the CEO, Renata Kowalczyk. Saad, meanwhile, was helping me, putting in a good word for me with everyone at the Wilmington Alliance who would have a hand in my hiring.

Renata Kowalczyk was the one responsible for bringing Second Chance into the Wilmington Alliance in the first place. She'd been approached by JP Morgan Chase, which had started the initiative and had reached out with grants to nonprofits around the country. When JP Morgan Chase asked Renata if the Wilmington Alliance would be interested, she didn't hesitate. She knew Saad and contacted him for help, and that's how my name ultimately entered the mix. The employer navigator position was obviously a brand new one, and she needed just the right person to fill it.

Renata had a soft spot in her heart for those whose freedoms had been taken away, whether through incarceration or otherwise. She'd grown up in Poland under communism. Her parents were freedom fighters, and she joined the underground herself when she was a little older. When she came to the United States, she flourished in the business world but never stopped looking for ways to help out those who needed a little boost, who needed some help getting around the barriers. The Wilmington Alliance was the perfect vehicle for her, and she was perfect for the Wilmington Alliance.

When we met, she seemed to like me right away. It didn't hurt that Dr. Wright-Smith had given her approval and Saad had recommended me to begin with. Renata liked my business experience, and she liked that I knew how to talk to those just coming out of prison. Mostly, she liked my body language. She told me later that in her time in the Polish underground, she'd learned that you couldn't necessarily believe what someone was telling you. By necessity, she learned how to read people. She picked up on my sincerity and eagerness to make a difference. "Welcome aboard," she said.

It had been a whirlwind. In a short time, I'd gone from that airport in Savannah, needing help from a TSA agent to navigate my way, to being part of something as important and gratifying as the Second Chance Employment initiative of the Wilmington Alliance.

I was on my way, and I was not looking back.

Meanwhile, while all of this was playing out, time flew by. The halfway house was followed by six months of home confinement. Home would now be my mother's house. I wore an ankle bracelet and had to check in every day when I got home from work. Now more settled, I started working on an old project. I started working on my memoirs again.

When home confinement ended, I turned in the ankle bracelet and began my five years of probation. After that I'd be completely free.

Or would I? Can a man ever be completely free of his past? More importantly, *should* a man ever be completely free of his past? For what is a man without his past, whether it be good or bad? We're all defined by who we've been and so, it seems to me, our past is not something from which we can ever really escape. Then again, it also need not be something that controls us, that stops us from moving forward.

In fact, it can serve as the opposite—a springboard to a better future. Kelli DiSabatino was right. It's about accountability and responsibility and, ultimately, about the legacy you want to leave.

The thing is, I already know the formula. I know how to get where I want to go. I know how to shape my future. I know how to leave the legacy I want to leave. I've known it for years. I learned it, and I was well trained on it. But now I can use that training for good instead of bad. I can take it deeper and use the formula I learned not for superficial, transient things, and not against other people. I can use it for the things that matter, the lasting things, the things that count. And I can use it not to better my circumstances but to better myself and to better those around me.

When it comes to my own mental state, my own attitude, my own perspective on where I'm going, I'm going to seek control. I'm going to move. And I'm going to dominate.

Epilogue

A life is a sum of the daily choices made. The choices we make shape the course of our lives in profound ways. Some good. Some bad. Either way, they carry consequences that ripple through time. Sometimes we see the consequences immediately. Other times, the consequences may not be realized for weeks, months, even twenty-two years.

Many of the choices we make are in pursuit of an often touted but ambiguously defined goal of "success," commonly portrayed as achieving security, wealth, or fame. We find ourselves striving relentlessly for this success, sometimes to our detriment. The pressure to succeed can create tunnel vision, blinding us to the broader aspects of a fulfilling life and dulling the senses to believe that as we climb the ladder of success, we become more and more immune to the consequences of our choices.

That's why it's important to take time to self-reflect and evaluate our choices before we act. Failure to invest the time before making even the smallest of choices can lead to significant problems. Rushed decisions, driven by impulsiveness or pressure, may cause us to overlook potential repercussions. Taking the time to weigh our options and seek advice is essential to ensure that our choices are made with clarity and foresight, minimizing the likelihood of regret or unforeseen complications.

From the ages of twenty-five to thirty-five, the choices I made were in great part influenced by society's perceptions of my success, leading me to an ego-driven life of superficial achievements instead of authentic satisfaction. I was living a lie, even lying to myself. The need for external validation and the pressure to conform to societal expectations overshadowed my personal intuition.

Ten years' worth of those choices led to twice that many years of incarceration and a reshaping of the rest of my life.

I realized almost too late that living a meaningful life was not accomplished by accumulating more and more money but required the alignment of my ambitions with my values to create a balanced existence that would prioritize personal growth, empathy, and a positive contribution to society. I say "almost" because it's not too late. I have a second chance. It's never too late for any of us.

We can start by redefining success to avoid the pitfalls of relentless ambition and materialism. We can instead embrace a journey that enriches our lives and the lives of those around us. We can make choices with authenticity and integrity, choices that will lead us to more meaningful paths in life. And choices that will create positive contributions to our communities and society as a whole.

My hope is that my life might serve as an example of, first, the consequences of bad choices and, second, the potential for redemption and the unbridled possibilities of better choices.

May all your choices be good ones.

Receiving certificate of completion from Judge Burke for participating in re-entry court

First time back to past location of the Orange Bowl Committee office

First time back at University of Florida

Reunited with high school track coach Bob King (middle) and teammate Mark White

Sharing a moment with Senator Tom Carper at Kingswood Community Center event

With Kingswood Board Chair James Rhodes and Senator Chris Coons

In a panel discussion with state senator Marie Pinkney (far right) on criminal justice reform

A special moment with Coach Mike "Mouse" Hollaway

Speaking at a press event about the impact of the Jackson Street Boys Club

With former mayor Mike Purzycki (right) and license commissioner Jeff Starkey

With Maryland governor Wes Moore during a criminal justice reform event at the Democratic National Convention

With Pennsylvania governor Josh Shapiro at the same event

With National Criminal Justice Reform leader Saad Soliman at the Future Ready Now convention. Saad's colleagues, Teresa Hodge on the left, and Laurin Leonard on the right.

With producer Omar Bradford and director Victorious De Costa

With state representative Sherry Dorsey Walker at JP Morgan Chase expungement event

With councilwomen Latisha Bracy and Wilmington Alliance CEO Renata B. Kowalczyk

With Renata at the Clean Slate National Convening

Sharing a moment with Delaware attorney general Kathy Jennings, Corey Priest, and Quincey Thomas at Project New Start graduation

With Delaware governor Matt Meyer at Project New Start graduation

With Wes Southall

Return of the Westside Connection:
Jeff Starkey, Steve Washington, me, and James Rhodes

Acknowledgements

My deepest appreciation goes out to *everyone* who has supported me over the years and stuck by me through the worst of times, but especially Kenny Neismith, Rachel Riley, Debra Mobley, and Paul White. You'll never know how much your support helped me carry on.

My sincere gratitude to those who have helped me tell my story. For your encouragement and input, thank you Dianne Ashford, Omar Bradford, Victorious DeCosta, Kelli DiSabatino, Hajji Golightly, Darryl Holsendolph, Renata Kowalczyk, Debra Mobley, James Ray Rhodes, Dr. Hara Wright-Smith, Saad Soliman, Wes Southall, Jeff Starkey, Keith Tribble, Steve Washington.

Special thanks:

To my co-author, Jerry Payne, for his professionalism, patience, and belief in this book.

To Leonard "Swan" Mason, for his vision, optimism, and dedication. (Sorry you came under suspicion, Cuz.)

To Nicky Boothe, for her judgement-free unwavering support, invaluable insights, and belief in this project.

Finally, to my mom for her never-ending unconditional love.

www.ingramcontent.com/pod-product-compliance
Lightning Source LLC
Chambersburg PA
CBHW020538030426
42337CB00013B/903